W9-AZX-572

The No-Nonsense Biblical Man

By Nate W. Holdridge

Thank you for your friendship. You
are a man to me.

The No-Nonsense Biblical Man
By Nate W. Holdridge

Copyright © 2013 by Calvary Monterey

ISBN-10: 1484053508
ISBN-13: 978-1484053508

Unless otherwise indicated, all quotations are from The Holy Bible, English Standard Version® (ESV®), copyright © 2001 by Crossway, a publishing ministry of Good News Publishers. Used by permission. All rights reserved.

Scripture quotations marked (NKJV) are taken from the New King James Version®. Copyright © 1982 by Thomas Nelson, Inc. Used by permission. All rights reserved.

All rights reserved. No portion of this book may be reproduced, stored in any retrieval system, or transmitted in any form or by any means without the express written consent of Calvary Monterey.

Printed in the United States of America.

Dedication

For my amazing wife, Christina, without whom I wouldn't understand manhood in the slightest.

For my beautiful daughters Lauren, Violet, and June. May you one day find a man like the one described in this book.

Table of Contents

Foreword

"You and I are going to read Pastor Nate's book!"

"Mom, this is a book for men, and we are both girls!"

"Yes, and we both like men and don't know how to pick them!!!"

This was the conversation between a mother and her teenage daughter at our church when Pastor Nate announced this book. In his comments, Nate mentioned that one reason he wrote *The No-Nonsense Biblical Man* was to describe the type of man he hoped his daughters would find in the future.

Simply put, this is a book that simply honors and elevates the healthy Christian man. I love that phrase "no-nonsense" because I hear so much absolute <u>nonsense</u> in secular and Christian circles about manhood, marriage, and raising children. I assure you: there is no nonsense in the very direct approach that Pastor Nate uses.

I am privileged to serve as an assistant pastor to the author, and I have seen him and his family in all manner of settings and situations. As a forty-year veteran of pastoral ministry and a father of four daughters myself, I have some level of experience in assessing a man's life, character, and family. This book is thoroughly biblical, and its message one that Nate is insanely serious about living out every day!

Please read this book slowly and carefully, and take courage. You can be (or *find*!) a wonderfully no-nonsense Biblical man!

Pastor Geoff Buck
January 2013

Preface: God Is Looking for Men

God is looking for men. *"For the eyes of the Lord run to and fro throughout the whole earth, to give strong support to those whose heart is blameless toward him"* (2 Chronicles 16:9). He is looking for God-fearing men, men he can work through and work with. He is looking for ordinary guys who are willing to take their walk with God seriously, willing to trust God in the details of life. He is looking for men He can develop into modern-day heroes, men who will be useful to their communities and the world and a blessing to their families and churches. God is looking for men.

This book could easily begin with a declaration that manhood is under siege. We could begin by citing the gender wars and cultural marginalization of the role of fathers as evidence that manhood is not what it used to be. I could give examples from pop culture that ridicule men by making us look moronic, shallow, and only about one thing. However, I want to say it like this: God is looking for men.

You really can't read the Bible without coming to the conclusion that God has a huge heart for men. Of course this means God has a general concern for mankind, men and women included, but it is also obvious God loves to work through men in a special and distinct way. Whether it is the responsibility He gives to Adam, the blessing He pronounces on the patriarchs, the role He delegates to Moses, the platform He builds for His prophets, the ministry He grants to His apostles, the order He outlines for His church, or the Savior He confers on the world, God is interested in working through men.

I believe this truth is timeless. I believe the God of Abraham, Isaac, and Jacob, the God of Peter, James, and

John truly desires to work through the lives of men today. He is looking for men who will live consecrated lives before Him. He is looking for men who will join in arms with one another in taking up the battle and cause of Christ. He is looking for warriors. He is looking for leaders. He is looking for lovers. He is looking for men to conform to the image of Christ.

As the pastor of a local church, I have watched the incredible influence of men in various settings and situations over the years. I have watched men launch ministries, plant churches, serve their families, and bless their world. I have also watched men suck ministries dry, split churches, destroy their families, and worsen their world. Men are that powerful, that influential. God is looking for men who will use their influence for His honor and glory. He is looking for men who will lead lovingly, tenderly, and sacrificially like Christ, blessing the world in which they live in the process.

And I do believe that manhood is under siege, by the way. I believe pornography, extended childhoods, an entertainment culture, the acceptability of shirking typical male responsibilities, and other elements lead to an overall reduction in real men in this world and culture. Enough is enough. "*For the time that is past suffices for doing what the Gentiles want to do, living in sensuality, passions, drunkenness, orgies, drinking parties, and lawless idolatry*" (1 Peter 4:3). I, for one, agree with Peter.

I long to write to men with a broken or misguided moral compass, to men who haven't grown up in a culture that reinforces biblical concepts and values, to men who have been doing life by a different playbook altogether, or have at least been taught to live that way. There is a new generation of men who don't have a biblical mentality embedded into them as a byproduct of culture, and I want to speak to them.

Now I should say I believe immensely in the plan of God for women. As the husband to an amazing woman—a woman I would not want to live without—and as a father of three daughters, I will contend earnestly for the roles and callings of God upon the other gender. To me, there is a reason woman was the final piece of God's creation, the crowning moment of God's created order. Together, men and women are made in the image of God. Without the other gender, that image is not fully seen. I don't hold this as a sentimental value, but as a biblical conviction.

That said, this book is written for and about men. However, it can also be read by women, particularly those women who would like to know more fully what a biblical man looks like. As a father of three daughters, I am hoping some women will read this book as well. In one sense, I am writing this book with my daughters in mind. They will likely marry someday, and my hope is that the men they marry are the kinds of men I describe in this book. So, although it is a secondary goal, my hope is for this book to help more women know a little more fully what a biblical, loving, Christ-like man looks like.

But since this book is primarily for men, I intend to take a fairly straightforward approach in this book. My goal isn't to write a lengthy treatise on biblical manhood, but to say what needs to be said. I would like to cut out the clutter, point to Scripture, and encourage men in the calling God has placed upon their lives. My hope and prayer is that men will actually read this book, so I'll keep it short and to the point. Not because I believe men to be dull or unintelligent—I don't—but because I believe we've got things to accomplish, goals to realize, and dreams to dream. Let's get to it. Let's cut out the nonsense and take a look at what God looks for in His men.

Chapter 1: Your Heart

"After this many of his disciples turned back and no longer walked with him. So Jesus said to the Twelve, 'Do you want to go away as well?' Simon Peter answered him, 'Lord, to whom shall we go? You have the words of eternal life, and we have believed, and have come to know, that you are the Holy One of God'" (John 6:66–69).

I'm a fan. A huge fan. A fan of men. I'm sure I could begin this book with some generic rant against the state of manhood and declare a battle cry against it, but you need to know I am a huge fan of men. Made in the image of God, men amaze me. When we are reconciled to this God through the blood of Christ, because we are made in His image, we become most capable. The potential inside the life of every single man is enormous. I see this all the time. Many men I know have tapped into God's best for their lives, and they are killing it. Absolutely killing it. And I believe God is looking for more men like them.

Yes, God is looking for devoted men. He's looking for men with grit, men who will serve Him and follow Him. He's looking for men of determination. Men who will worship. He's looking for guys who are willing to put more than a nominal effort into their walk with Him. He is looking for men who are crazy about Jesus. He is looking for men who take their spirituality seriously. It is more than a sideshow to them, more than a Sunday routine, but something they stand for. It drives their lives and their motivations. Men like this draw a straight line from the cross of Christ to their everyday lives. And God is looking for more men like this.

God is looking for men like Joshua. I'm sure it's the war stories, but Joshua has long been one of my favorite biblical characters. He comes onto the biblical scene as Moses's young and trusted assistant. When Moses would finish his "face to face" meetings with God, Joshua would stay behind in the tent, presumably to linger in the presence of God (Exodus 33:11). Joshua was devoted from the start. After Moses's death, Joshua assumed leadership in Israel. He stepped into Moses's place, which would have been an intimidating position for any man, and I'm sure Joshua struggled with his fair amount of fears. This seems evidenced in Joshua 1, where God had to encourage him three times to "take courage." But Joshua was a devoted man. He had made up his mind. He urged the men in Israel to make up their minds as well. *"And if it is evil in your eyes to serve the Lord, choose this day whom you will serve, whether the gods your fathers served in the region beyond the River, or the gods of the Amorites in whose land you dwell. But as for me and my house, we will serve the Lord"* (Joshua 24:15).

It is important for the issue of allegiance to be settled in the mind of God's man. You see, for men like Joshua, the issue has already been determined— they know who they will follow. They belong to God, and God belongs to them. God is craving men like this today. Men with guts. Men of determination. Will we take God and His word seriously? Or will we live a lukewarm "Laodicean" kind of life (Revelation 3:15–16)? The choice is ours, and, like it or not, this is a choice that will stay with us for all of eternity.

Be Gospel- Centered

It all starts with the Gospel. Far too much teaching on the life of a Christian man centers around the actions of his life instead of on the heart that beats within him. The no-nonsense biblical man must have a deep-seated heart for the Gospel. His life must have been radically affected by the Gospel message. We will of course look long and hard at the man of God and how he lives his life, but without the Gospel message embedded inside his soul, how will this man have any motivation to serve and love God?

I can remember years ago sitting in a Bible study listening to a pastor teach from the book of Ephesians. Week after week this particular pastor emphasized the "grace of God." In the naivety of my heart I longed to move past this simple message. At that point in my life, the Gospel was something you learned in children's church by way of the multicolored bracelet where each color represents a different part of God's redemptive story. In my mind, maturity meant moving past the Gospel. The Gospel was simple and childish to me. What a fool I was.

One day the pastor referenced Ephesians 1:3 — "*Blessed be the God and Father of our Lord Jesus Christ, who has blessed us in Christ with every spiritual blessing in the heavenly places.*" He explained to us our great and incredible position in Christ. He explained to us that in a past sense we had already been given every blessing that is found in the heavenly places. He detailed for us how this was acquired, not by our own doing, but by being placed in a position called "in Christ." I began to understand, at that moment, that the Christian life isn't so much about doing as it is about receiving.

From that moment on, I've seen my own life and works as a simple response to the Gospel. I see my life and all that I do in obedience to God as a simple thank you note for what he has allowed me to receive. This motivation has been crucial to my staying power. I am very certain that without this wonderful Gospel message being cemented into my heart I would not be walking with God today.

One place we see this principle laid out for us is in Titus

2:11–14. *"For the grace of God has appeared, bringing salvation for all people, training us to renounce ungodliness and worldly passions, and to live self-controlled, upright, and godly lives in the present age, waiting for our blessed hope, the appearing of the glory of our great God and Savior Jesus Christ, who gave himself for us to redeem us from all lawlessness and to purify for himself a people for his own possession who are zealous for good works."* In other words, grace trains us for a certain type of life. Contrary to the beliefs of many, grace does not lead us into a life of licentiousness. According to Paul, a true understanding of the grace of God leads us to a godly life filled with heavenly passions—a life of self-control, integrity, and purity. This life can be described as zealous. A man who has discovered the truth of the grace of God is a man on fire.

I don't know exactly what it will take, but you absolutely must get the Gospel deep inside your heart. This is non-negotiable. Jesus must become famous to you. His work on that bloody cross has to become so fascinating that it stirs your everyday life. If this doesn't occur in your heart, you will either be a mere shadow of who you could be, a sort of Christian zombie going through the motions, or you will be stuck with a spiritual-looking but plastic, artificial, and hypocritical version of Christianity in your everyday life.

Perhaps you are already there. Perhaps your passion for the Gospel is flowing nicely. Perhaps you are currently overwhelmed with the forgiveness, cleansing, and eradication of shame that Jesus has offered you. But maybe the Gospel has never been fascinating to you. Maybe you've drifted through the years away from an adoration of Christ and His Gospel. It's time to come home. Although I will write more about these specific areas later on in this book, I'd like to give you a few suggestions on how to fire up your love for the Gospel.

1. Find Gospel-Centered Friends

Birds of a feather flock together, as they say. But you're not a bird, and you can choose whom to hang out with. You could form your primary male relationships with those who are opposed to Christ, those who are lukewarm to Christ, or those who are passionate for the Gospel. One great way to develop a Gospel-centered heart is to choose the latter, men who love the message of the cross. Men often resist this, but I encourage you to get into small groups and intentional relationships with other men who appreciate Jesus deeply. You may feel awkward talking about Him at first, but friendships with strong believers and conversations with them are vital. I will never forget the first time I sat down on a weekly basis with a small group of men to support and pray for one another. Game-changing.

2. Listen to Gospel-Centered Teaching

"Faith comes from hearing, and hearing through the word of Christ," scripture tells us (Romans 10:17). Whether we like it or not, there is power in preaching. Consider Titus 1:2–3—*"in hope of eternal life, which God, who never lies, promised before the ages began and at the proper time manifested in his word through the preaching with which I have been entrusted by the command of God our Savior"* (Titus 1:2–3).

The proclamation of the word is very important to our Christian vitality. That said, there are many different styles of preaching today. If you have a cold heart toward the Gospel, or if it isn't alive inside your heart, I would encourage you to make sure you are listening to Bible teaching that is absolutely Gospel-centered. If Jesus, His cross, and His atoning work are the central theme of the messages that you hear, then you are likely listening to Gospel-centered messages. If you are coming away with tips and suggestions on how to live a better life, if the theme of the message is you and not Christ, then you are likely not sitting under Gospel-centered teaching.

3. Read the Bible in a Gospel-Centered Way

Another way to develop a Gospel-centered heart is to resist the temptation to read the Bible as if it is a book all about you. It isn't. The Bible is designed to communicate who God is to this world and His plan to redeem that world. Everything in the Bible, from Genesis to Revelation, points to Christ (Revelation 19:10). If we only see the Gospel in the Crucifixion accounts, then we aren't reading the Bible intelligently. See "Jesus vs. Sin" in "David vs. Goliath." See how the Spirit of Christ rebuilds a human life when reading the rebuilding project led by Nehemiah. See Jesus's willingness to reconcile with men who betrayed Him in the life of Joseph, a man who was willing to reconcile with brothers who betrayed him and left him for dead. Search for the Gospel in every portion of scripture you read.

It's all about Jesus. This is the bottom line of what I'm trying to communicate. The no-nonsense Biblical man must be a Jesus guy. There has to be a love for Him and devotion to Him wrapped up in this man's life. Jesus is central to his thoughts, dreams, perspectives, and priorities. This will not turn this man into a Ned Flanders lightweight kind of a man, but into a devoted man. This will not make him out of touch or impractical, but will instead give him an excellent filter with which to view all of life.

Identity in Christ

The man of God has a Gospel-centered heart, but he also finds his identity in Christ. Recently, while I was speaking on the subject of our relationship with God, someone asked me what God brings to this relationship. In other words, we might know some of the practices we will hold to that strengthen our walk with God, things like Bible study, prayer, and fellowship, but what does God actually do in this mutual relationship? It is a great question which necessitates a manifold response, but one of the principal actions of God in our relationship with Him is to pronounce identity. He declares who we are.

This, after all, is what good fathers do. Good fathers will speak into their children's lives and give them a healthy outlook and identity. When a father says "well done," "I like it when you…" or "what I see in you is…" his children will likely be listening. This is a shadow of the work of the original Father, God, who identifies and speaks into the lives of His children.

God pronounces a wonderful identity upon those who have received Jesus. For those who have embraced the work of Christ on the cross of Calvary, believing and trusting in His blood for their redemption and cleansing from sin, the Father makes wonderful declarations about us. Forgiven, redeemed, cleansed, and adopted are some of the words that come to mind. The greatest declaration of all, however, is not so much an action but a position. The Father has placed us in Christ. This is our new identity.

In Christ is a wonderful place to live. As I referenced earlier, Ephesians 1:3 speaks of our current standing in Christ. Because we are in Christ we already have received every spiritual blessing in the heavenly places. I live in Him and He in me. I am one with Christ. As one pastor friend of mine put it, God has cut and pasted the life and righteousness of Christ into my file. I am closely identified with and associated with Him.

At Jesus's baptism, when the Holy Spirit descends and the Father speaks and says, *"This is my beloved son, in whom I am well pleased,"* I have the same standing. I am in Christ. When the Father looks upon my life, He sees me as He sees His own son.

Here are a few of the blessings we have in Christ, as found in a few of Paul's epistles. In Christ we have redemption (Rom. 3:24). In Christ we are dead to sin and alive to God (Rom. 6:11). In Christ we have eternal life (Rom. 6:23). In Christ there is no condemnation (Rom. 8:1). In Christ there is freedom from the law of sin and death (Rom. 8:2). In Christ we are inseparable from the love of God (Rom. 8:29). In Christ we have grace (1 Cor. 1:4). In Christ we are already raised and seated with God in heaven (Eph. 2:6). In Christ we have been brought near by the blood (Eph. 2:13). In Christ we have Jesus's humble mind (Phil. 2:5). In Christ we have righteousness (Phil. 3:9). In Christ our minds are guarded by peace of God (Phil. 4:7). In Christ we have provision (Phil. 4:19).

The more a man understands his identity in Christ, the better. Some of us had decent fathers, while many of us did not. Either way, it is far better to receive identity from the perfect heavenly Father than it is to receive identity from any flawed earthly man. I would never diminish the role of fathers, and later in this book I will talk about the importance of fatherhood, but receiving our identity from our Father God is of paramount importance.

One reason discovering this identity is so important for the Christian man is that it is the ultimate insecurity killer. Men struggle with insecurity like crazy. It manifests itself in many ways, including pride, chauvinistic exploits, sexual escapades, lack of confidence, false bravado, absentee leadership in the home, and endless boyhood. But the man who becomes satisfied with who he is in Christ and his great position in the sight of God and who allows that identity to sink into his soul, becomes able to resist these symptoms. His heart is healthy, so the need to act out in these ways has been greatly decreased.

Quite often a man's insecurity will lead him to various forms of idolatry. The false security he feels worshipping at the altar of sexual immorality, for instance, is often a direct result of his lack of understanding or awareness of his identity in Christ. Paul felt this way when he asked the sexually immoral Corinthians, "*Or do you not know that your body is a temple of the Holy Spirit within you, whom you have from God? You are not your own*" (1 Corinthians 6:19). Apparently a deeper understanding of their identity as present-day temples of the Holy Spirit would have helped them discern the error of their ways sexually.

I know this is a man's book, but the woman at the well in Samaria is a wonderful example for us to consider (John 4). Jesus offered her living water which would satisfy her soul. She misunderstood Jesus's offer, instead looking for physical water. Jesus then pointed out her five previous husbands and a current live-in boyfriend. These relationships made it painfully obvious she was thirsting for something greater. And we follow suit. We thirst and we hunger, but when we do not allow Jesus to be our satisfaction, we inevitably turn to lesser things to satisfy our lives. This is why the subject of identity is so important. If a man can discover his identity in Christ and become satisfied in it, he becomes an altogether different man.

I wanted to make sure to harp on this near the beginning of this book for the simple reason that it is easy for a man to find his Christian identity in his actions. But before we become Bible-reader-man, church-going-man, or family-man, we must be a man who sees and knows himself in Christ Jesus. This is not a position we are able to earn. Only the blood of Jesus could earn this position for us. We receive it by the grace of God.

Transformed through Relationship

Once the man of God falls in love with the Gospel and begins finding his identity in Christ, he is ready to become transformed by God through relationship with God. Perhaps you've heard the line "it's not about religion, but relationship." So true. That said, I believe the devoted man will cultivate a daily walk and relationship with God. Perhaps this sounds awkward at first, but God is calling and drawing us into fellowship and community with Him. He has worked hard to restore what was lost in the Garden of Eden, a friendship with Him that was constant, open, and without shame. Jesus spoke of an intimacy with Him that is closer than any earthly relationship: *"Whoever feeds on my flesh and drinks my blood abides in me, and I in him. As the living Father sent me, and I live because of the Father, so whoever feeds on me, he also will live because of me"* (John 6:56–57). The fellowship the Son experienced with the Father is the example Jesus used to describe the abiding relationship we can have with Him.

Obviously, an entire book could be written on our daily relationship with God. And while I do want to touch on subjects like prayer and Bible study, it's important for me to start out with a grander theme. My simple fear is that we so easily lock onto the externals of relationship, things like where, when, why, and how. We tend to look at the "how-tos" of a walk with God, instead of simply understanding this new covenant relationship He has called us into.

A great place to start would be 2 Corinthians 3. There Paul explains the difference between the glory of the Old Covenant relationship with God, a glory which was passing away, and the never-ending, never-fading, and everlasting glory of the New Covenant relationship with God. He calls the law-based relationship with God the *"ministry of death"* and compares it to the cross-based relationship with God which he calls *"the ministry of the Spirit."*

He talks about Moses's experience under that Old Covenant relationship. Whenever Moses would go into fellowship with God, his countenance would visibly change. There was an apparent afterglow left upon his face. However, the problem was that this afterglow would inevitably fade. It couldn't last. It couldn't produce lasting change. It wasn't real transformation.

Juxtapose this with the Gospel-based New Covenant relationship with God, Paul tells us. In this relationship there is a possibility of real and permanent transformation. *"And we all, with unveiled face, beholding the glory of the Lord, are being transformed into the same image from one degree of glory to another. For this comes from the Lord who is the Spirit"* (2 Corinthians 3:18). This is absolutely wonderful and, without attempting to oversell this, life-changing. Let's discover how to enjoy this relationship with God piece by piece by taking a closer look at each phrase of 2 Corinthians 3:18.

With Unveiled Face

In this New Covenant relationship with Christ, we are able to come to Him with an unveiled face. Moses brought a veil with him to meet with God. He would remove the veil during his meeting times with God. Upon exiting the tent, however, Moses would reinstall the veil over his face. We do not approach God in this way. As believers, we have an all-access pass to God. We come boldly before His throne of grace. We aren't there solely because of our wonderfulness, but because we are positioned in Christ. His righteousness has become our positional righteousness. This gives us great boldness before the Father. Additionally, and more importantly to Paul's point, we don't have to put the veil back on after we spend time with God. As opposed to the temporary change Moses experienced, this change is lasting and permanent in nature.

"Beholding the Glory of the Lord"

This is Jesus. Jesus is the *"glory of the Lord"* Paul is referring to in this phrase. To behold Him is to have an intimate and personal relationship with Him. This is studying Him in His word, crying out to Him in prayer, and worshipping Him from our hearts. This is fascination with who He is and His glory. Change comes by interacting with Him. Every time you take off that mask and get before Jesus by opening your heart to His word and hearing His voice minister to you, you are beholding the glory of the Lord.

"Are Being Transformed into the Same Image"

God's desire for us is to transform us to become more and more like Jesus. This word "transformed" is not an oft-used biblical word. It is used to describe Jesus's transfiguration in places like Matthew 17, and it is used to describe the process we are able to go through with His help. To understand this transformation process, another helpful English word would be the word *metamorphosis*. As we behold Christ with an unveiled face, we morph into His image. We become like Jesus.

Contrast this with many of the messages delivered to Christians today. *"You must change. You better grow. You've got to get this right."* Certainly, every believer has a part to play in this process, and we'll get to that in a moment, but the transformational nature of our relationship with Christ should not be neglected or overlooked.

"From One Degree of Glory to Another"

This speaks of a process. Our daily relationship with Jesus will produce gradual growth in our lives. Slowly but surely, we become more and more like Jesus. I can look back upon my own life and see certain periods of transformation. It is a myth that by simply aging we become sweeter and kinder. Our respective childhoods, educations, and natural demeanors will give each one of us a different starting point, but we all have immense room to grow. I'm sure the people in our lives would appreciate us behaving a little more like Jesus and a little less like our natural man.

"This Comes From the Lord Who Is the Spirit"

The Spirit of God is the one who actually produces the change within us. In another place Paul writes, *"For the one who sows to his own flesh will from the flesh reap corruption, but the one who sows to the Spirit will from the Spirit reap eternal life"* (Galatians 6:8). Sowing to the Spirit through an ongoing relationship with God will produce results.

One place this is exemplified is in the life of David. Called and anointed by God, David was different from the rest. When the soldiers in Israel's army trembled at Goliath's taunts, David stepped to the forefront, believing and trusting God for the victory. This win propelled him into the public spotlight and fame, which awakened the insecurity and jealousy within King Saul's heart. As a result, David eventually fled for his life. One of his first hiding places was the cave of Adullum. While there, a large band of men gathered to him. These were men who were distressed, discontented, and indebted under Saul's regime. We can also assume that many of them were present for the taunts of Goliath, too afraid to move a muscle. They weren't natural warriors who trusted in God.

Near the end of David's life, however, an accounting is given of the mighty men who surrounded David. These men carried out great exploits, killing giants, predatory animals, and large bands of warriors. They were brave, seemingly invincible. Clearly, the God of David had made Himself available to these men as well.

What happened to these men? How did they transform from a weak and scared collection of men into an elite fighting force? I believe the major change was the time they had spent in David's presence. Simply put, a relationship with David had left them altered. Just as knowing a giant killer like David is bound to change you, a relationship with Jesus Christ is bound to transform a man. The character and nature of Nate isn't going to change Jesus, but the character and nature of Jesus is bound to transform Nate.

Jesus desires to change and transform your life through relationship with Him. He is longing to flood your heart with His word, hear your cries ascend to Him, and interact with you daily. As you do, He will transform your life. This is the walk of faith—trusting and enjoying a God we cannot see with our eyes and believing this relationship will change each one of us for God's glory.

Let Him In

The man whose heart has been set on fire by the Gospel, who finds his full identity in Christ, and who develops a transformational relationship with God, will begin to discover an amazing brand of life. This kind of man allows Jesus truly and deeply into his heart. He is intensely in love with the Gospel of Jesus Christ. He is passionate for the work of Jesus on the cross. This man is intensely aware of the beautiful position he has found in Christ Jesus. He does not work to obtain the grace of God, but instead he receives it. His entire life is lived in gratitude to God— a sort of thank you note in response to the treasure God has blessed him with in Christ. This man is transformed by the Spirit of God into the image of Christ through his daily relationship with Him. He longs for the nature of Jesus to become realized within his own life. His heart has been changed. A fuse has been lit within his heart, and an explosive work of God is in store.

Chapter 2: Your God

"And in that day, declares the Lord, you will call me 'My Husband,' and no longer will you call me 'My Baal'" (Hosea 2:16).

To some degree, arranged marriages have to be slightly awkward, especially when the young couple has little to no previous knowledge of one another. Everything would be brand new. Interests, personalities, and values would be yet undiscovered. I mean, who is this new person you are going to live the rest of your life with? Does this person have a sense of humor? Is this person someone who likes to be alone or prefers to be with people? What drives and motivates this person? Is he or she lactose-intolerant? Is this a person who likes Hawaiian pizza? Without being an expert on the subject, I imagine those first few years are difficult in many ways.

There has to be a similarity in our relationship with God. Without pressing the analogy too far, we kind of jump right in to our new relationship with Him. Perhaps a pastor or a friend told you it was wonderful, and, as stated earlier, it was promised to be a relationship, not a religion. It sounds so great. Still, you get this thing started, and it can be awkward to know where and how to begin. So the God who created the universe desires an intimate relationship with me, huh? Where do I begin? How is this supposed to go down?

Don't worry. This isn't an exact science. God is mysterious in many ways (Romans 11:33-36). There are depths to Him we will explore for eternity. To put a friendship or relationship with Him in a box would be foolish. To put rigid lines around what a relationship with Him looks like would only set us up for disappointment, comparisons, and serious fatigue in our walk with Him. We know we get there through the blood of Christ, and we know there are currently various means made available to tap into His grace, but like any relationship, there will be a significant ebb and flow over the years in how it all works for us. My goal isn't to put a fine edge on anything, but to loosely examine the more significant ways God desires to interact with us.

I've often heard people refer to the beginning days of their walk with God as their "first love." They usually describe a period of immense joy, often demonstrated through the free sharing of their faith with others, lengthy Bible reading sessions, and seemingly endless worship services. If this has been your experience, you know what I'm talking about. Pure joy. But over the years, I've discovered the beginning isn't like this for everyone.

Perhaps all this is so brand new to you that everything from attending a church service to reading a Psalm is a stretch. Maybe you started off well, but have hit a dry stretch. I hope to help you as we begin to look at our relationship with and to God. Remember, He loves you and cares for you. If you are in Christ, your position in Him is secure. He is longing to help you by transforming you into the image of His Son. Here are some ways this simple relationship with Him can occur.

Love

"And he said to him, 'You shall love the Lord your God with all your heart and with all your soul and with all your mind. This is the great and first commandment'" (Matthew 22:37–38).

Jesus declared boldly that the greatest commandment is to love God with everything you are. Simply put, any talk of a relationship with God must involve a deep love for God. We saw this in the last chapter in reference to being a Gospel-centered man. Still, it bears repeating. This is a love relationship that we are in.

By loving God we are not completing God. God is self-sufficient and in need of nothing. Before the world was created, the Triune God existed and lived in perfect joy and gladness. Sometimes people describe God as a needy figure who desperately craves our love because of what it does for Him, like He's this little puppy dog in the sky that will whimper and whimper until we pet him. I'm not really looking to worship a god like that. Our God is self-sufficient, almighty, the beginning and the end. Still, make no mistake, He does crave our love, but He craves it for our benefit, not His. By design, since we are made in the image of God (Genesis 1:27), the act of loving God produces incredible health in our lives. In short, to love God is the deepest of benefit to our human souls.

This love for God inoculates us from many of the dangers men face in life. Common sins like covetousness, lust, and hatred are prevented through a deep love for God. David, when repenting of his sexual sin with Bathsheba and murder of her husband Uriah, understood this. He confessed, "*I have sinned against the Lord*" (2 Samuel 12:13). He had slipped in his walk with God and became vulnerable to temptation because he had neglected his deep love for God. David had a love for God that had previously and would again govern his life, but in that moment he cared not for God and found himself willing to sin against Him.

This is one reason why I've encouraged you to have a deep appreciation for the Gospel. I find the quickest way to rekindle my love for God is to meditate upon the Gospel of Jesus Christ. When I consider His great love for me, what He has accomplished for me, and the free gift that is mine in

Him, my heart begins to once again overflow with love and thankfulness toward God.

When establishing this in your life, it is important to remember this reality: you will look different from every other man. You have your own journey to walk in order to develop your love for God and appreciation for His Gospel. For me, this initially occurred from age eighteen to twenty. I began attempting to walk with God near my eighteenth birthday, but found deep difficulty in doing so. Habitually, I turned back to my old sin, which wasn't that old at the time. Then and there I decided to attend a small Bible college in order to "sit at Jesus's feet" for a couple of years. This was essentially a Christian camp-type experience where I weekly came face-to-face with God and His grace toward me. This foundational time revolutionized my life by embedding a pure and real love for God deep inside my heart.

My path is in no way a template. In fact, I made many friends while in that little Christian camp-type Bible college who have since abandoned God. Apparently, for them that season did not cultivate a love for God, but rather a distaste for God, although it shouldn't have. My goal is simply to emphasize the importance of having a deep love for God embedded inside your heart, not to introduce a template. An appreciation for God begins it all. Just as love is central to marriage and family, so is love central to our relationship with God. His love for us is clear in the cross, but it is important for our love for Him to become real and firm, foundational to who we are.

Worship

"Worthy are you, our Lord and God, to receive glory and honor and power, for you created all things, and by your will they existed and were created" (Revelation 4:11).

Another factor in your relationship with God is worship. When Jesus taught His disciples to pray, he gave them what we call the Lord's Prayer. Inside of that prayer is a fascinating little line that goes like this: "*Your kingdom come, your will be done, on earth as it is in heaven*" (Matthew 6:10). This portion of the prayer is especially interesting when one considers what we know of heaven. What is happening in heaven? What does life look like there?

John, in writing the book of Revelation, which, as the name implies, was a received revelation from God, was caught up into the throne room of God in heaven. There, he found worship. The angels and the elders were continually exalting and praising God.

An extension of love, worship is ascribing honor and worth unto God. Again, this doesn't complete or add anything to God, but recognizing God for who He truly is and honoring Him for it adds something to us. Better yet, it restores something to us. We are more in line with what God created us to be when we are caught up in worship of Him. When worship invades our hearts, it affects our priorities, goals, and dreams.

Although worship does include the singing of psalms, hymns, and spiritual songs (Ephesians 5:19), it goes far beyond music. It is an attitude, a reverence, a sense of honor. It can be found in prayer to God, conversations with a friend, or in our personal thoughts. Whatever the vehicle, it is important for men to develop a worshipful heart.

A worshipful heart is a relieved heart because it has placed God on His rightful throne, and it no longer senses a need to be in charge or have everything under control. A worshipful heart is a healthy heart that doesn't need to lash out in anger or jealousy. A worshipful heart is a balanced heart where priorities are finely tuned and idolatry is crushed. I find my heart set free and infused with peace when I realize afresh the magnitude of my God, His sufficiency and love, His ability and sovereignty, and His wonder. There is something healthy and good about seeing God more clearly for who He is and responding to that vision.

I would encourage you to develop a worshipful heart through various means, many of which I will write about briefly. Learn how to sit before God and recount His grace upon your life. Learn how to walk before Him and admire His attributes, many of which we will never experience. Omniscience, omnipotence, and omnipresence, for instance. Rejoice in His wisdom, glory, love, kindness, justice, integrity, sinlessness, and mercy. Think of His character as you find it in His word and honor Him for it. What follows are a few practical ways to cultivate this heart of worship.

1. Writing

Simply jot down as many of His attributes as you can think of, pausing to write or say aloud your praise concerning each one. What about His power is majestic to you today? What impresses you about His foreknowledge today? How does His faithfulness toward us in the sun, moon, stars, and seasons move you today?

2. Singing

It is much easier to mindlessly sing a song to God than it is to engage your heart and mind with the lyrics. Think about the lyrics when group-singing with other believers. When alone sing songs and hymns that challenge you. Singing has been a part of God's community in every biblical age, so it is important to sing with intelligence and passion to God. Something unlocks in my heart when I give myself to this. In one place during their wilderness wanderings, the people of Israel sang to the rock in order for water to flow (Numbers 21:16-18). There are times when the water of God's Spirit becomes unleashed during and after I've sung to God.

3. Fellowship

Sincere admiration of God can be wonderfully expressed in conversations with other believers. Praising God to others is a great way for worship to increase. Telling your wife or children of God's goodness is pleasing in His sight. Perhaps a grumpy or disillusioned heart simply needs to tell others of the goodness and greatness of God.

4. Silence

Our digital age makes silence something we have to fight for. Even when quiet, our minds are nearly always on the move, but periods of quiet before God, thinking about Him and speaking to Him, are healthy ways for a man to have a growing appreciation for who God is. I often accomplish this through the solitude of a long hike or prayer walk.

Years ago I discovered my tendency to derail, to freak out, during times of trial. I would find myself losing trust in God. I would inevitably attempt to take the reins back and try to control my own life. One practice would always help. Alone with God, I would begin to recount to Him everything He had done for me, everything I could remember and knew about, at least. I would simply move down the timeline of my life, sometimes starting at the very beginning, and would worship Him for His faithfulness in my life. I would confess that He had truly used all things together for good (Romans

8:28), even events I couldn't make sense of yet. Slowly I would find my heart lifted up into true worship of God. Sanity would return to my mind. Peace would again enter my heart.

This kind of event has replayed itself a thousand times. Whether during a worship service, a sermon, a Bible-reading session, a conversation with a friend, or a time alone with God, my bearings are gained once again as I worship God. His worth is beyond compare. He is your God, and He is a God worth praising.

His Word

"Blessed is the man who walks not in the counsel of the wicked, nor stands in the way of sinners, nor sits in the seat of scoffers; but his delight is in the law of the Lord, and on his law he meditates day and night. He is like a tree planted by streams of water that yields its fruit in its season, and its leaf does not wither. In all that he does, he prospers" (Psalm 1:1–3).

Love and worship are important when it comes to our relationship with God, but He has also given us His word as a way to interact with Him. I would never expect anyone in my life to relate to me without my word. Every relationship I'm in, whether it's with Christina (my wife), one of my three daughters, a fellow pastor, a friend, or a member of the congregation, hinges upon the words we speak to one another. I would anticipate someone learning about me by observing my actions, but to really know me one would need to listen to my words.

In one sense this is why Jesus is called the Word (John 1:1–3, 14). He expresses and explains God because He is God. *"No one has ever seen God; the only God, who is at the Father's side, he has made him known"* (John 1:18). In other words, the best way to understand and discern God is to look into the face and cross of Christ.

However, God has also given to us an abundance of words that enable us to know Him. The sixty-six books that form the Bible are a wonderful way to discover and know God intimately. No relationship with Him is complete without it. I cannot say I know my wife without actually listening to her explain her heart. No matter how close I feel to her, I have got to hear her word and understand it in order to know her. Likewise, it doesn't matter how close one might feel to God, without His word, that person is missing a look into His very heart and will. A friendship with God necessitates a deep appreciation for His word.

I've always thought the psalmist nailed it because he clearly lays out the bottom line. At the end of the day, the man who rejects the counsel of the ungodly, instead delighting and meditating on the word of God, will be the blessed man because of all the fruit coming out of his life (Psalm 1:1–3). Everyone loves a fruitful man because their lives are improved by knowing him. Wives, children, friends, girlfriends, churches, coworkers, comrades, overseers, and many others are benefitted by the fruit from this man's life. Who wouldn't want to be a man of the word?

I long for you to know the word of God. I have been blessed with the opportunity to study the Bible as part of my job since I was twenty years old. It has been a wonderfully edifying experience. I am thankful to God for putting me into a church family that appreciates expositional teaching at all levels of the church. Still, nothing could replace my personal time studying the Bible for my own benefit. I need it desperately. My marriage, family, friendships, and church family are better off when I am consistently in the word on a personal level. Since I believe the same for you, here are some ways your time with God's word might be helped.

1. Read

The psalmist declares a blessing is found through delight and meditation upon the word of God, but delight and meditation begin with reading. Too often Christians will sit down with their Bibles and treat them unlike any other books they've ever read. Notepads, highlighters, commentaries, and websites are helpful, but don't let them clutter the simple reading of God's word. Three chapters in the Old Testament and one chapter in the New Testament daily will enable you to read the Bible through in about one year's time. Perhaps you enjoy moving more slowly through God's word. Excellent. I would still encourage you to designate other times to simply sit and read at a quicker pace as it will help you discover the flow of the Bible more easily.

2. Write

For me, simply jotting down a word, phrase, prayer, or principle in response to what I just read in scripture is an incredibly edifying practice. I find the message of the Bible reinforced in my heart as I write down the things I'm seeing in His word. I try to keep it brief, as lengthy commenting only slows my time in His word, but writing has been a standard part of my Bible reading since the very beginning.

3. See God

Unless you were born with a seminary degree, there will be much in the Bible that does not make sense to you as you first read it. Additionally, there will be much that does make sense to you, but doesn't seem to be highly applicable to your own life. While reading, I've found it helpful to look for the attributes and characteristics of God in any text I'm reading, especially when reading at a faster pace. There is always something to learn of God in the text, and this, after all, is what the Bible is about.

4. Find Jesus

Although difficult in some passages, I would encourage you to try and find the connection with Jesus in any portion of scripture. Most Bible passages are preparing for the Gospel, foreshadowing the Gospel, declaring the Gospel, or teaching about the results of the Gospel. As stated before, seeing how all scripture points to Jesus is a wonderfully edifying experience. Attempt to find Him in every passage.

5. Listen

I have been greatly aided over the years by the audio teaching from various pastors and teachers. Modern technology has enabled vast amounts of teaching to be stored on an iPod or thumb drive. In many cases, the Internet has rendered storage pointless as the teaching can all be stored online and streamed to your device. With the technology you own, find good Bible teaching that will enable you to accelerate your pace of learning.

Our church, like many churches, utilizes the Android and iTunes app store markets to distribute our weekly teaching via our own church app, as well as through our website and weekly podcasting. My suggestion is to go beyond merely listening to other churches' sermons and series, however, and find through-the-entire-Bible teaching or through-one-book-of-the-Bible teaching that will enable you to learn the different books of the Bible better.

Prayer

"And he was teaching them and saying to them, 'Is it not written, "My house shall be called a house of prayer for all the nations"? But you have made it a den of robbers'" (Mark 11:17).

A love for God, the worship of God, and interaction with the word of God are all important in our relationship with Him, but now we come to the subject of prayer. Volumes have been written about prayer. It is difficult to move through even a few chapters anywhere in God's word without coming across the subject of prayer. In other words, God appears obsessed with prayer. From the front to the back of the Bible, God appears as a Father who longs for His children to cry out to Him in prayer. He appears as a lover who desires his wife to call out to him in prayer. He appears as a sovereign who calls his people to petition him.

There is an interesting event in Jesus's triumphal entry into Jerusalem, the week before He was crucified, that has always stood out to me. It's a rather climactic event and moment in His life, but after Jesus rides into Jerusalem, receiving the praise and adoration of the people along the way, He enters into the Temple Mount. Mark tells us, *"He entered Jerusalem and went into the temple. And when he had looked around at everything, as it was already late, he went out to Bethany with the twelve"* (Mark 11:11). In a rather anticlimactic move, Jesus simply looked around the temple, observed everything, and departed. On the following day, He saw a fig tree and expected to find fruit upon it. Being hungry and finding no fruit, Jesus then cursed the fig tree, which immediately withered and died. The next scene shows Jesus in the temple once again driving out the money changers and those buying and selling in the temple precinct, making a profit off the people, and taking advantage of them. In this moment He cries out, "*Is it not written, 'My house shall be called a house of prayer for all the nations'?*" (Mark 11:17)

The two scenes are clear. The fig tree is simply a picture of what was happening at the Temple Mount. There appeared to be fruitfulness, what with all the sacrifices, smoke, and commotion, but Jesus "looked around at everything" and couldn't find any fruit. Just as He rebuked the fig tree, so He rebuked the activity there at the temple. A place that was supposed to be known for the fruit of prayer was instead a prayer-less place. The smoke ascending was supposed to indicate their rising cry to God, but instead only illustrated their dead religiosity. But Jesus was looking for prayer.

So we find that God is looking for men who will cry out to Him. He is looking for men who will express their dependence upon Him through a life of personal and passionate prayer. Here are some simple ways to urge and encourage your prayer life along.

Pray out loud. Praying out loud helps us remember this is simply a conversation with God. Additionally, I find that a distracted mind is helped through audible prayer.

Pray silently. There are often times where it is good to remember that we are praying to an invisible God who knows our thoughts. Silent prayers enable us to, perhaps, pray more quickly, earnestly, and spiritually than when our prayers are verbalized.

Pray with others. Praying to God with others is a true joy for a Christian man. Holding up each other's burdens, agreeing with one another's requests, and opening up our hearts in front of others is a tremendous blessing. I only wish more Christians would discover this timeless joy.

Pray while walking. Some of my most deeply impactful moments in prayer have occurred while walking. I find early morning, late night, or wilderness paths best suited for mobile prayer, but I have also been known to encircle my dining room table on cold winter mornings when the outdoors or my garage just won't do!

Pray while kneeling. While there are many different postures included in the Bible, kneeling or bowing before God is common. Indeed, there are moments when the casual nature of walking or sitting cannot sufficiently communicate our hearts. Likewise, there are times when the drifting heart needs to snap back into allegiance by bowing the body before God.

Make a list. I would encourage you to produce a prayer list from time to time. Far from a rigid document that one must pray from, if it is created thoughtfully and prayerfully, it should be a wonderful stimulant into deeper areas of prayer. Additionally, one finds great encouragement at seeing God move in a particular prayed-for area.

Just do it. The best way to learn how to pray is to simply pray. We can theorize and study all day long, but until we get out there and attempt to pray, we will never learn. And, rest assured, we are always learning.

One of the most difficult ways to learn about prayer is through a book. For me, I've found one highly effective way to learn about prayer is by praying with other people who know how to cry out to God. I learned about prayer by watching the life of my father. He was a man who would spend every morning in prayer. I'm certain he wouldn't describe his prayer life as perfect, but it served as a wonderful example to me. Later in life I had the opportunity to pray in a group with him. His adoration and worship, but especially his devotion to the kingdom of God and a relentless unwillingness to pray for silly things in his prayers served as a wonderful template for me. Through him I was able to see prayer for the gift it is.

This deeply personal act ought to be a part of every Christian man's life. I believe God hears our prayers, keeps our prayers, and appreciates our prayers (Revelation 5:8). I believe He moves in response to our prayers, even though how this all works out and combines with His sovereignty is a deep mystery to me.

Trust

"By faith Enoch was taken up so that he should not see death, and he was not found, because God had taken him. Now before he was taken he was commended as having pleased God. And without faith it is impossible to please him, for whoever would draw near to God must believe that he exists and that he rewards those who seek him" (Hebrews 11:5–6).

"For we walk by faith, not by sight" (2 Corinthians 5:7).

We can love God, worship God, read God's word, and pray to God all day long, but eventually we all have to trust Him more. Any good relationship requires an element of growing trust. Our relationship with God is no different. Because God is spirit and therefore invisible to us, our walk with Him is based on faith and not sight. We lean upon the

God we cannot see and choose not to trust the elements we can see. As the psalmist wrote: *"Some trust in chariots and some in horses, but we trust in the name of the Lord our God"* (Psalm 20:7).

In most of our lives our trust in God is very small at first. Some of us might be willing to get out of the boat and walk to Jesus, but most of us choose to stay in the boat (Matthew 14:33). So when I talk about trust in God, I'm not talking about some natural temperament certain men possess. No, instead I'm talking about a growing sense of dependence and trust in God, an ever-developing sense that God is trustworthy, able to be depended on, and our greatest ally. Some of us may come embedded with serious trust issues when it comes to God, while others may more easily lean upon Him. *What I'm stressing, however, is the importance of possessing a growing, developing, and improving trust in God.*

Make no mistake, this does not come naturally to us. Again, some speak of the development of our trust in God as an inevitable process that comes with age. I have met plenty of men much older than I am who have yet to even begin trusting God. Their entire life is held together through their own wit, ingenuity, and effort. They know God like they know their barista, so they have never started trusting Him wholeheartedly. They might know how to take calculated risks in the business world, but they have yet to learn how to take risks with and in God.

No, our natural tendency is to trust self. This sense of control makes us feel safe and protected. But simple mathematical analysis of our ability compared with the ability of God should tell us that God is worth being trusted. I love to use the best case vs. worst case scenario grid to help clarify decisions I need to make. What is the best case scenario if I trust God completely? What is the worst case scenario if I don't? What is the best case scenario if I trust myself completely? What is the worst case scenario if I don't? I think the upside that comes with trusting God is immense. Our families, friendships, cities, and churches will be better off if they are filled with men who trust God more than they trust themselves.

Now, just because it isn't an inevitable process doesn't mean it isn't a process. Indeed, as with any relationship, learning how to trust God takes time, experience, and testing. But make no mistake, God is worthy of our trust. Great things occur when we lean upon Him and place our faith in Him. Without trust the ark is never built in Noah's day, Jerusalem is never repaired in Nehemiah's day, and the church is never built in the apostles' day.

One of the greatest examples of biblical trust is found in the life of Abraham. Abraham had received wonderful promises from God, but these promises would be tested in his lifetime. Even though he had believed God, and God had accounted his belief to him for righteousness, there was still the inevitable testing of that belief (Genesis 15:6).

Since the promise of God with Abraham required he have a male child, the testing of his faith often involved his offspring. During one season, long before he and Sarah ever had a child together, Abraham was tested with a proposal by his wife. Although shocking to our modern sensibilities, she proposed they have a child together through her maidservant Hagar (Genesis 16:2). This was a test. Would he trust God or depend on his own abilities? Would he lean on God and believe His promises or attempt to work things out for God? During this season of Abraham's life, his faith in God faltered. Instead of trusting that God would provide offspring for him through Sarah's womb, he took matters into his own hands and trusted himself to get the job done. What followed in the birth of Ishmael was problematic for generations to come.

This is what happens when we take matters into our own hands. When we refuse to bow the knee to God, cultivate a worshipful heart toward Him, and develop a relationship with Him, we will inevitably take matters into our own hands. When we do, the people in our lives are doomed. Sometimes the results are minor, other times the consequences are cataclysmic; but either way, everyone involved would be better off if we had simply trusted God. Men who are able to trust God with their sexual impulses, their priorities, and their finances are few and far between, but men like this are an incredible blessing to the people in their lives.

Later on in his life, however, Abraham became one of the greatest examples of trust found in the history of God's people. Eventually God had given him and his wife Sarah a wonderful son named Isaac, thus fulfilling His promise of a child through Sarah (Genesis 18:10). Abraham treasured this miracle baby and Isaac became his favorite son. God promised the blessing He had declared over Abraham would be extended to and through Isaac (Genesis 21:12). One day God tested Abraham by asking him to take his "only son" Isaac and sacrifice him on Mount Moriah (Genesis 22:2).

At first glance this test sounds horrible and gruesome, but a wider scriptural lens reveals a God who would never ultimately require this sacrifice from Abraham, but would volunteer it for Himself. In other words, our heavenly Father didn't ultimately ask Abraham to sacrifice his son, but did send His only begotten Son to die for the sins of the world. As grotesque as Abraham's test from God may seem at first glance, in reality it should cause us to appreciate the Gospel all the more. God was willing to do that which seems awful to us.

That said, Abraham passed this test with flying colors. The same man who had taken matters into his own hands in the situation with Hagar and Ishmael was willing to trust God completely during this next season of his life. He heard the word of God and obeyed the word of God. He did not argue, make excuses, or disobey. He submitted and trusted completely.

I imagine Abraham struggling with two seemingly irreconcilable statements from God. On the one hand, God had promised the blessing would flow through Isaac's life, but Isaac had yet to have children. On the other hand, God had asked Abraham to take Isaac's life. He knew God had spoken both statements, and it was impossible for him to reconcile the two. How would both of these statements work out? Hebrews gives us an insight into how Abraham was able to pass this test. *"He considered that God was able even to raise him from the dead, from which, figuratively speaking, he did receive him back"* (Hebrews 11:19).

Abraham believed that if he had to go through with it, taking Isaac's life, God was duty bound to raise Isaac from the dead. Before he'd even heard of anyone being resurrected by God, he trusted God for a resurrection. That is some serious trust! But this is where God desires to take our trust. When presented with two seemingly opposed truths, our duty is to trust God by obeying His clear command for us. Let's briefly consider how trust plays out in a few pertinent areas of a man's life.

Time

Although logic might tell me that I need to work and earn money seventy-plus hours per week, God's word tells me that I need to place a priority on worship, service, and family. Certainly God's word commands us to be hard-working and diligent men, and there are definitely seasons where our work patterns will be more intense, but as a lifestyle, we must trust God with the priorities of our time, believing He will be faithful to provide for us.

Finances

We will discuss giving and finances later, but suffice it to say God has asked us to be a generous people. Giving and generosity ought to flow from our lives. That said, every gift we give, every tithe check we write, and every donation we make is a miniature test of our faith. Do we believe what Paul told the generous Philippian church, *"And my God will supply every need of yours according to his riches in glory in Christ Jesus"* (Philippians 4:19)?

Spiritual Disciplines

Giving ourselves to spiritual disciplines like Bible study, prayer, service, and fellowship requires a deep amount of trust. Instead of practicing these disciplines, I could experience more entertainment, earn more money, or enjoy more sleep. When trust in God comes in, I believe my life will be filled with more joy, my future filled with more reward, and my heart filled with more rest as a result of these practices.

Future

The future is one intensely difficult area for men to trust God with. I wonder how many times I've missed out on a wonderful opportunity from God because of my lack of trust and faith in Him. I believe countless men have missed God's calling upon their lives because they cannot trust Him for it.

One way this is exemplified is our insistence on a bolt of lightning experience as a prerequisite to serving in our local church, while a mere ability with numbers will qualify us for a lifetime career in accounting. God must move land and sea to tell us to serve Him, while we choose hobbies, jobs, and interests based on basic impulse. While I understand the need to take the callings of God seriously, something doesn't seem right about this.

God is looking for men who will trust Him completely. Again, this will surely develop over time. Some of my earlier "victories" of faith seem so introductory as I look back upon them, just as I am sure I'll see many of my "great steps of trust" as rather novice in the years to come. But at the moment you pass through them, they are all a big deal. Lean upon Him. Remember His cross. He is truly trustworthy.

Submit to God. Trust God. Lean upon Him. Our love of God, worship of God, study of the word of God, and prayer to God must culminate in submission to God. Obey and trust. Trust and obey. It does no good to have a worn-out Bible filled with notes and highlights if we refuse to obey God.

Jesus said, *"Beware of the leaven of the Pharisees, which is hypocrisy"* (Luke 12:1). Just as everyone appreciates a bountifully fruitful man, everyone looks down upon a man who has a spiritual look and feel to him, yet a complete lack of trust, submission, and obedience to God. If God is truly worthy of our worship, if He is the authoritative God of heaven, and if His interest in us is always for our good, then it follows that He has earned our obedience. God isn't in the market for *spiritual-looking men*, but *truly spiritual men* who are consecrated unto Him in every area of life. In the coming chapters, we will take a look at our relationship to things and people outside of us, as well as the struggles inside of us. Our submission to God's will impacts every single area of our lives.

God Longs for You

"I am the vine; you are the branches. Whoever abides in me and I in him, he it is that bears much fruit, for apart from me you can do nothing" (John 15:5).

Make no mistake, men, God is looking for a deep and abiding relationship with you. An intimate relationship with God is not reserved for the women in our families and churches. The bravest and greatest men in human history demonstrated a deep connection with God the Father. Our ultimate example of this is found in the life of Jesus Christ. Jesus said, "*I and the Father are one*" (John 10:30). He did nothing outside of His connectivity to his heavenly Father. He was always about his Father's business. Jesus actually prayed for us to experience unity with Himself in a way similar to His experience with the Father (John 17:20–23).

He describes our relationship with Him as an abiding relationship. Just as the branches continue in the vine and receive all of their life and nutrients from the vine, so Jesus longs to provide us with the life we need as we continue in relationship with Him. He longs to pour his life out into yours. He longs to make you more like Him. He longs to strengthen you, enable you, and make you fruitful in this life. This fruitfulness is only found through a strong relationship with God.

Go on this journey with God. "*Oh, taste and see that the Lord is good*" (Psalm 34:8)! Enjoy Him. Partake of Him. Let Him be the father, husband, sovereign, and leader He longs to be in your life. The dividends are endless.

Chapter 3: Your Mission

We are instructed to run to win. *"Do you not know that in a race all the runners run, but only one receives the prize? So run that you may obtain it"* (1 Corinthians 9:24). In other words, in the Christian life it isn't enough to simply show up. God is looking for men who will run hard, men who will give it everything they've got.

If you've ever been in a race, you understand the importance of preparation and the importance of taking it seriously. If you show up on race day carrying extra weight on your body or if you find yourself easily fatigued, you have no one to blame but yourself. Your lack of training, dedication, and commitment held you back from your peak performance. I believe God is looking for dedicated men— men who are committed to the process of sanctification and are of the kingdom of God. I believe you and I are called to be such men.

That said, I believe we often rush to talk about areas of potential growth in a man's life before addressing the larger picture of calling. Now, I believe fully that God is looking for instruments that are clean vessels he can use, but I think quite often we forget to talk to men about the general call of God upon their lives. Sanctification for sanctification's sake could be perceived as boring, but sanctification for the honor of the cross and the glory of God is exciting.

In other words, when a man discovers his calling, or even that there is such a thing as the calling of God, he gains passion and motivation for the process of sanctification and growth. There is a desire, a reason, a goal. He longs to be sanctified and clean and pure because of Jesus and His blood, but also so that he might be available to the calling Jesus would lay upon his life.

Calling

"For we are his workmanship, created in Christ Jesus for good works, which God prepared beforehand, that we should walk in them" (Ephesians 2:10).

There is nothing like being used by the God of the universe to help someone, nothing quite like serving God. Each one of us has been called to serve Him; each one of us has been called into the ministry. I long for a day when the term "layperson" is eradicated from our vocabulary. For me, the term conjures up images of a clergy working hard while a large group of people "lay" around and do nothing. Who wants to be part of a church where you don't get to get your hands dirty? This isn't the exciting Christian life God's men have been called to. Instead we ought to chase the calling of God upon our lives, making sure not to disqualify ourselves through sin, staying fresh in our relationship with God, and going for it.

With certainty we can say there is an order in the church, the body of Christ. We know God has given spiritual leaders to serve His church, as a gift from God to His people (Ephesians 4:11). Still, we must not lose sight of the mission of such men. Their everlasting goal is to *"present everyone mature in Christ"* (Colossians 1:28). Part of this maturity comes by equipping believers for ministry work, so they are able to build up the body of Christ (Ephesians 4:11–12).

Paul explained to the Ephesian church how God *"gave the apostles, the prophets, the evangelists, the shepherds and teachers, to equip the saints for the work of ministry, for building up the body of Christ"* (Ephesians 4:11–12). In other words, the spiritual leaders work hard to teach, instruct, prophesy, exhort, and communicate God's word in order to equip God's people for His work. Paul wrote this to the Ephesian church, and I believe Paul discovered this principle while in Ephesus serving Christ and planting churches.

Never staying long in any of the cities he ministered in, Paul served the Ephesians for a comparatively long period of time (Acts 19:8–10). When he arrived there, he followed a slightly different format of ministry. Because it was the opportunity afforded to him, Paul took a small group of believers aside and instructed them every day in a school building he had rented for the purpose (Acts 19:9). As a result, the Ephesian church grew strong, biblical, and active. They took the mission of God to heart, and within two years' time, all of Asia Minor heard the word of God as a result of this church (see Acts 19:10). In Ephesus, Paul was willing to equip God's people for their calling; and this group of people was also willing to embrace the calling of God upon their lives.

This is all-important to the Christian life. By studying God's word, continuing steadfastly in prayer, and engaging in true Christian community, we are enabled to a greater degree for all God wants to do through our lives. He will forever be the one working through us, but by learning, surrendering, and growing, we are simply submitting ourselves to Him and His work.

How about you? Have you embraced the simple reality that God desires to work through your life? We live in a broken and hurting world. There are people to reach, churches to plant, and hearts to restore. The God who was willing to leave the comfort of heaven for our benefit is looking for men who are willing to engage in His mission.

Jesus said, *"Blessed are those who mourn..."* (Matthew 5:4). Is there something within you that mourns over the condition of the world? I'm not talking about political frustrations or anything like that, but a deep hurt at the isolation of man and a consciousness of the love of God. In a million different ways, God wants to work through His men. I believe a generation of men will rise to this challenge. They will go forth boldly, consecrating their time, treasure, and talents for the living God.

Part of the journey for every man of God is discovering his calling. We know we have been *"created in Christ Jesus for good works"* (Ephesians 2:10), but where and how, specifically, should we serve? I believe every man ought to learn of the "good works" God desires to prepare him for.

Recently I went through the edifying process of creating a personal mission statement. After years of teaching the Bible and pastoring God's people, I had a fairly decent understanding of God's heart and desire for me. Still, I wanted to see if I was missing anything. I didn't want my scope and vision to be so large that I lost out on effectiveness. Over the course of a month, I prayed through and pondered the passions, gifting, talents, and interests I felt God had given to me. I considered Bible passages God had used in my life in a significant way. I thought about how God had used me in the past. I considered experiences I've seen fruit in. I thought about action words I like best. I noted themes and prayed through it for a while. In the end I was able to boil it down to a simple statement something like this: *Nate Holdridge is called to communicate scripture, build up men, and launch ministry.*

I can't tell you how helpful this clarifying statement has been to me. My goal isn't to get you to create a mission statement for your life, although at some point that may be helpful to you, but to illustrate the joy of having some marching orders from God. With the end goal of clarifying your calling, let's observe a few of distinct areas of your life. This evidence might enable you to see the bigger picture for your life more clearly.

Interests

Taking inventory of the interests and passions of your heart is helpful in discovering your calling. What do you get excited about? Are you interested in helping underprivileged children? Does your heart beat with leadership principles you want to pass down to the others? Perhaps you have a deep desire to see health inside of families or have a passion for fatherhood. Every Christian should have the desire for evangelism, but perhaps your heart for the lost is stronger than most.

Understanding what you are passionate for is very important to understanding your ministry calling. Practically speaking, passion cannot always be the driving force that causes you to continue on in ministry; many times grit and determination are the factors at play, but passion sure doesn't hurt. It is difficult to serve God in an area you aren't passionate for. When I first started walking with God, I became immediately interested in ministering to high school students, a heart I carry with me to this very day. Perhaps that kind of ministry sounds terrifying to you. Either way, finding some of your interests and passions in ministry is invaluable. Just as a child who loves music will find it easier to stick with piano lessons, so the child of God who loves convicts and their families, for example, will find it easier to go on prison visits. Without passion and interest, a ministry like that might make you so nervous you lose your lunch.

I encourage you to get alone with God and allow Him to search your heart regarding the areas you feel strongest about. When you read the news, what causes your blood to boil? When you are surrounded by large groups of people, who do you naturally gravitate toward? What great problem would you love to help fix?

Talents

Taking a look at your talents is another way to unearth some of your potential callings. Each one of us has talents and abilities that we have acquired over the years. Some of your talents will be more obvious, such as the abilities you've acquired in order to carry out your profession. Whether you're a chiropractor using your ability to create an open door for the Gospel in El Salvador, a teacher giving English lessons along with the Gospel in Czechoslovakia, or a mechanic helping the single mothers of your local church, our professional abilities can be redeemed for God's purposes. Ask yourself, how could the talents I've acquired over the years be used for the glory of God?

Two words of caution, however. First of all, we need to understand that by performing our duties well, earning a living, and carrying out our profession to the best of our ability, we are already using our talents for the glory of God. In other words, we don't necessarily have to use our talents for a direct ministry purpose in order for God to receive glory from them. Every part of our work should be done as unto Him. *"Whatever you do, work heartily, as for the Lord and not for men"* (Colossians 3:23). Secondly, I would also caution against thinking your secular occupation is what you ought to be doing in the church world. Perhaps you are a high-powered businessman with wonderful leadership abilities. That doesn't necessarily mean that God wants you to be a leader in the church. Perhaps He desires for you to serve children inside the church, knowing this would best suit you and them.

Beyond our professional talents are other abilities that, at first glance, seem less significant than what we do for a living or are simply part of what we do in our job place. Ability with numbers could lead to helping families in your church figure out their personal budget. A knack for planning and organization could lend a helpful hand to a church planter who is trying to get a new fellowship off the ground. Even some athletic skill, like the ability to play basketball, could lend itself to ministry as you coach children in your community, many of whom are fatherless and in need of good role models. When seen from this angle, there are ministry opportunities all around us.

Gifts

Interests and talents are one thing, but spiritual gifting is paramount when it comes to the calling of God upon our lives. The Holy Spirit gives spiritual gifts to His people. I believe this. "*Now there are varieties of gifts, but the same Spirit; and there are varieties of service, but the same Lord; and there are varieties of activities, but it is the same God who empowers them all in everyone*" (1 Corinthians 12:4–6). The Bible lists gifts of prophecy, service, teaching, exhortation, generosity, leadership, mercy, words of wisdom, words of knowledge, faith, healing, miracles, distinguishing between spirits, tongues, interpretation of tongues, helps, administrations, and evangelism (see Romans 12, 1 Corinthians 12).

My goal isn't to give an exhaustive list, nor is it to scare anyone who has never studied the Holy Spirit and His gifts, but to simply state that we must do the ministry of God by the power of God. It is one thing to have natural abilities, interests, and talents, but it is another thing entirely to be gifted by the Spirit of God for the work of God.

I'm very thankful because, early on in my Christian life, while attending the small Bible college I alluded to earlier, one of the first experiences I had in that school was a small class on the subject of the Holy Spirit. Before taking that class, I would have referred to the Holy Spirit as an "it" or a "force," but I likely would never have really thought of Him as the third person of the Trinity. Biblically, He has a will, He loves us, He can be grieved, He is jealous for us, and, as Paul stated regarding the gifts, He "*apportions to each one individually as he wills*" (1 Corinthians 12:11). It was during my time in that small class that I fell in love with the Holy Spirit of God. I began to realize He could and would walk with me and talk with me. He would energize me and empower me for this life. On top of all that, He would strengthen me for the ministry He had called me to.

Perhaps it will sound fanatical to you, but one night in particular stands out in my mind. I was reading Chuck Smith's book *Living Water*, an excellent book about the Holy Spirit and his gifts that I would recommend today for a fuller understanding regarding the Holy Spirit, when I sensed the Spirit of God impress something on my heart. Pastor Chuck told a story about a time when had pleaded with God to receive other gifts of the Spirit. He then sensed God speaking to him something like this, "I haven't called you to those other things; I've called you to teach my word." When I read that line, it was as if the Spirit of God was speaking those words directly to my own heart.

Keep in mind I was only eighteen years old at the time. The last thing I wanted to do was teach the Bible. At that time I didn't know what it would mean for me to teach the Bible; the pastorate was the furthest thing from my mind, but I realized I might end up teaching children, youth, and adults the word of God in some kind of setting. It didn't matter that I didn't have the details at the time (I still feel like I don't have all the details!); I was so glad to have sensed a little of God's direction for my life. God had begun to show me one of the gifts He would put in my life, the gift of teaching.

Now, the last thing I'm trying to do is convince you that

you must sense a strong impression from God in order to do anything in His kingdom. In fact, most of the gifts and callings God has put in my life have not come via a still, small voice or powerful impression. No, through simple observation, I've been able to discover gifts of leadership, ministry, and others. Additionally, there have been many times God has given me a word of wisdom or knowledge, but I wouldn't characterize myself as having the gift of the word of wisdom or knowledge. To me, God simply loaned those gifts out for the moment I absolutely needed them. God has simply chosen to intervene at different moments in my life and help me by the power of His Holy Spirit. No, all I'm trying to communicate is the paramount importance of receiving gifts from the Holy Spirit in doing the work of ministry. We must do His work in His strength or else we are toast.

Burdens

On top of all this, God will place burdens upon your heart. These burdens help clarify the callings of God upon you. A burden is simply a load to carry, like with an ox or mule. God will take a responsibility, care, or people and place them on your heart to carry. He will give you an unexplainable passion that cannot and will not die. Perhaps in a vision or a dream, but quite often in a simple quiet moment, God will grant you His heart. At times the burden is temporary, but often you will live the rest of your life with a deep-seated concern or ache for those people or that ministry. It is from God. You cannot shake it.

Years ago I was leading a small, fledgling, young adult Bible study. It wasn't flashy, cool, or reaching all that many people. It was simply a small band of brothers and sisters coming together every week to study God's word, pray, and fellowship together. One night, while driving to our meeting, I was singing in my car along with a worship album I had playing on my stereo. I can't remember which song was playing, but at that particular moment I felt like God gave me a vision. Out of the blue and all of a sudden, as I was driving and singing, I saw a room full of young people with their hands raised to the Lord in passionate praise and worship. I sensed God was showing me a bit of what He was going to do in my life. The love of God was so heavy upon me in that moment that I began to cry. I was overwhelmed with a burden from God, a burden that hasn't left me to this day, a burden to see young people electrified in their love for God. These aren't everyday occurrences, but ask God to open your heart to the burdens He longs to give you.

Sacrifice

"And calling the crowd to him with his disciples, he said to them, 'If anyone would come after me, let him deny himself and take up his cross and follow me. For whoever would save his life will lose it, but whoever loses his life for my sake and the gospel's will save it" (Mark 8:34–35).

Make no mistake, receiving your calling is going to take sacrifice. If I could say it like this, in many ways this is going to hurt. When Jesus answered the calling upon His life as the second person of the Trinity, it cost Him greatly. It was painful. It hurt. If we're going to follow in our Master's footsteps, we are going to have to experience a little bit of sacrifice, a little bit of pain, a little bit of self-denial. Still, Jesus promised us intense blessing if we would come after Him, deny ourselves, take up our cross, and follow Him. When we lose our lives for His sake and the Gospel's, we actually find our lives.

I think many times we love to root for the underdog. Think

about it. We tend to love the small, competitively disadvantaged athlete. When we see his hard work, diligence, and determination, we are inspired. On the other hand, when we see a physically gifted specimen of a man who simply doesn't put in the effort or the work required, we are disappointed.

As God's men, we have a wonderful opportunity. On the one hand, through our frailties and the weakness of our flesh, we are like the smallish, disadvantaged athlete. On the other hand, by the grace and mercy of God, through the gifts of enabling given to us by His Holy Spirit, we are like the gifted athlete. We have a wonderful opportunity. By adopting the mind of Jesus, the one who took the form of a bondservant and suffered death on a cross, we will live sacrificial lives. As Paul stated, "*Have this mind among yourselves, which is yours in Christ Jesus, who, though he was in the form of God, did not count equality with God a thing to be grasped, but emptied himself, by taking the form of a servant, being born in the likeness of men*" (Philippians 2:5–7).

Living life this way is an incredible paradox. Logic tells me that if I fight for my time, my agenda, and my priorities, I will be satisfied and blessed in this life. However, after pursuing all of those things with reckless abandon, I end up feeling empty, fatigued, and shallow. It is the strangest thing. When I scratch and claw to get mine, I end up miserable and frustrated. When I defy my own logic, however, and lay down my time, treasure, and talents for others and for the kingdom of God, I end up refreshed and recharged. Living life as Jesus taught us to live it leads to incredible blessing. If you have spent any time pouring into the life of another, you know exactly what I'm talking about. The reward is all yours.

I don't know what that first or next step is going to look

like for you. Perhaps you need to start giving, and we'll talk about that later on. Maybe you need to open up your home for a community group in your church. Perhaps you need to begin donating your musical talents back to God. Perhaps you've been living a sacrificial life for years. Let me encourage you, and by faith I believe you would encourage me, to lay down your life more and more for the kingdom of God and the cause of Christ. The rewards are truly eternal.

Sanctification

"For this is the will of God, your sanctification..." (1 Thessalonians 4:3).

Some instruments must be clean. When I use the tools in my garage, I usually am not all that concerned about their cleanliness, but when eating at a popular restaurant, clean utensils are pretty important to me, to say the least. It is the same in the work of God. God wants to work in and through your life, but he is looking for clean vessels, men who have set themselves apart from sin in order to love and serve their God. He is a holy God who says to His people, *"You shall be holy, for I the Lord your God am holy"* (Leviticus 19:2). Since Jesus went through a brutal death and the harsh experience of atoning for our sin, we should *"go out from their midst, and be separate from them, says the Lord, and touch no unclean thing"* (2 Corinthians 6:17). In an age of compromise amongst God's people, it is good to remember God's implicit call to come out of a life of sin.

Once a man begins to develop a relationship with God, he will immediately begin to discover potential areas for growth within his life. God is perfect. We are not. Spending time with God will reveal some cracks and flaws in our character. Just as hanging out with people of low moral character will decrease our standards, so spending time with Jesus is bound to raise the bar quite a bit. As discussed earlier, it is by *"beholding Jesus with an unveiled face that we are transformed into the same image from one degree of glory to another by the Holy Spirit of God"* (2 Corinthians 3:18 paraphrase mine). As we spend time abiding in Jesus and in relationship with Him, we are inevitably transfigured to become more like Him. He takes us through a metamorphosis of sorts, one in which His life is infused into ours.

This is good. As Paul writes, God's desire for us is sanctification (1 Thessalonians 4:3). It is one thing to be positionally changed, but God desires to practically grow us. He longs to develop our faith and purify our lives. He is looking for men to work in and through, so He desires to sanctify our lives for His glory. Again, this transformation only serves as a blessing to us and those around us.

So, when we think of sanctification we must ask who is responsible for our sanctification? Our first answer is to believe that it is God who does the sanctifying. The work of sanctification is primarily a work of God, so Paul prays, *"Now may the God of peace himself sanctify you completely"* (1 Thess. 5:23). The Father God *"works in you, both to will and to work for his good pleasure"* (Phil. 2:13). Jesus is our *"righteousness and sanctification and redemption"* (1 Cor. 1:30). The Spirit of God grants us the *"fruit of the Spirit"* (Gal. 5:22-23) by taking us through *"the sanctification of the Spirit"* (1 Pet. 1:2) and the *"sanctification by the Spirit"* (2 Thess. 2:13).

That said, God's men play both a passive and an active role in their own sanctification process. It could be said that God and man cooperate together in sanctification. As we yield to God and enjoy our relationship with Him, we then passively receive His benefits, including growth and transformation. However, there is an active participation we are to engage in. A simple observation of the major portions of the New Testament that are instructional should serve as ample evidence that God desires our participation. We are encouraged to pray, stay in the word, decide daily for God, and develop godly habits. As Paul wrote to the Philippian church, "*Work out your own salvation with fear and trembling, for it is God who works in you, both to will and to work for his good pleasure*" (Philippians 2:12–13). The Philippians already possessed salvation, so Paul encouraged them to work it out and express it through the energy of God. He knew they were a redeemed people, so he encouraged them to evidence their redemption by the way they lived.

Chapter 4: Your Consecration

"Before I formed you in the womb I knew you, and before you were born I consecrated you; I appointed you a prophet to the nations" (Jeremiah 1:5).

I've intentionally told you about our *calling* and *service* as men before getting into this section regarding our *consecration* as men. I feel quite often the bar is set low for us as Christian men. When we discuss sanctification, the first and only things we often address are sexual purity, anger, and pride. Obviously, we all understand why these subjects need such strong emphasis today. Men inside the church are being decimated by sin left and right. The Bible, to be certain, spends a great deal of time exhorting men and women in these particular areas.

The fear I have, however, is that if our goal is only to gain victory over temptation, then eventually men will grow bored in this Christian life. If all a man is called to is a placid, sterile form of living, he may eventually drop it all and turn to a life of sin out of sheer boredom. I think it is good for a man to wrestle with things like calling, passion, and gifting. A man's soul is fed as he engages in the mission of God.

That said, integrity and victory over sin are incredibly important subjects in the Christian man's life. There are some best practices that will keep and preserve a Christian man, enabling him to grow in grace and ability in Christ. In a word, this next section is all about consecration. Now, I understand consecration is a word we don't really throw around in everyday use, but it is an intensely biblical word.

Used most often in the Old Testament, consecration speaks of setting something apart for a specific purpose. The usual biblical usage concerns people, places, or things being consecrated unto the purposes of God. Whether it was the priests for the service in the tabernacle, the candlesticks for use inside the temple, or even Jesus himself, consecration speaks of people and elements which have been set aside for the purposes of God.

Not only were they set aside, but they were cleansed. There was a purification that took place. It was understood these elements and people would not be defiled by sin or any unclean thing. God desires to consecrate His men. He longs to see you and I separated unto Him, cleansed from sin, never to go back to the old life.

This was God's heart for the first murderer, a man named Cain. Cain had grown jealous of the favor God had shown his brother Abel. God had rejected Cain's sacrifice, but had received Abel's sacrifice. As this jealousy marinated within Cain's heart, God approached him with a word of exhortation and warning. *"The Lord said to Cain, 'Why are you angry, and why has your face fallen? If you do well, will you not be accepted? And if you do not do well, sin is crouching at the door. Its desire is for you, but you must rule over it'"* (Genesis 4:6–7). God longed to see Cain win victory over his flesh. He wanted Cain to take dominion over sin. He wanted Cain to be consecrated unto Him. Alas, Cain lost this battle and murdered his brother.

Near the end of the Bible, a woman and a city called Babylon are destroyed (Revelation 17–18). Personally, I believe they represent the false religious undercurrent and the world system operating behind-the-scenes, pulling at the hearts and minds of men and women to follow in its diseased purposes. No matter how you interpret this section of scripture, other Bible passages make it abundantly obvious there is a world system which attacks and blinds the hearts of men. John wrote: *"Do not love the world or the things in the world. If anyone loves the world, the love of the*

Father is not in him. For all that is in the world—the desires of the flesh and the desires of the eyes and pride of life—is not from the Father but is from the world. And the world is passing away along with its desires, but whoever does the will of God abides forever" (1 John 2:15–17). This pull and attack against mankind is very real.

God, after foretelling of the coming destruction of this world system, cries out to his people, *"Come out of her, my people, lest you take part in her sins, lest you share in her plagues"* (Revelation 18:4). From Genesis to Revelation, God has longed to see His people gain victory over sin. There is a war against our souls, a strong and inexplicable evil desire to disobey God and to be lord of our own lives. But God warns us because He loves us. He longs for us to be consecrated unto Him.

I agree with Peter when he writes, *"For the time that is past suffices for doing what the Gentiles want to do, living in sensuality, passions, drunkenness, orgies, drinking parties, and lawless idolatry"* (1 Peter 4:3). Why live as if the blood of Christ hasn't changed the game? Since God longs for His men to be consecrated unto Him, it is sometimes shocking to see the loose attitudes so many of God's professed children express toward sin. They live with girlfriends, abuse substances, and live frivolously without even a second thought. That said, I believe many people have a heart to be obedient to God, but have grown up in a culture that is so far from Him they can't even begin to pretend they know what His will is. The Holy Spirit is certainly able to directly teach His children and direct them through conscience and His word, so I would like to take a moment to teach and instruct on a few areas of the consecrated life.

Integrity

"Whoever walks in integrity walks securely, but he who makes his ways crooked will be found out" (Proverbs 10:9).

A man of integrity, a man with a strong moral compass, a man embedded with moral uprightness, is a gift. I call him a gift because I think some would often have us believe otherwise. Pop-culture, various forms of media, and school campuses often promote sinful behavior as virtuous, lavishing praise and honor upon the loosest, crudest, and most perverse. The man with morals and integrity is seen in a negative light. This is nothing new. Isaiah saw this in his own day: *"Woe to those who call evil good and good evil, who put darkness for light and light for darkness, who put bitter for sweet and sweet for bitter!"* (Isaiah 5:20). But God is looking for men who will honor Him and follow Him, even when no one is looking, and even when it isn't fashionable.

I believe you will be one of those men. I believe the Spirit of God is drawing you, speaking to you, and convicting your heart. I believe you want to live a consecrated life full of integrity. As brothers, it is vital we encourage one another to live a consecrated life. Your relationships and the world will only benefit as you live this kind of lifestyle.

I know firsthand how difficult it can be to "come out of the world." As I stated earlier, I attempted to walk with God when I was seventeen years old. For nearly a year, I failed in the face of common temptations like sexual license, substance abuse, and partying. Even in the times I didn't want to live this way, I found myself reverting to old habits and practices. I agreed with Paul before me who said, *"For I do not understand my own actions. For I do not do what I want, but I do the very thing I hate"* (Romans 7:15).

This is not a season of my life I am proud of, a regrettable season I still wish I had never gone through. While in it, I was absolutely miserable. I had little moments of victory, but for the most part I was flailing and failing in the Christian life. Do you know what did the trick, what enabled me to finally find some victory? Separation. Separation gave me the space God needed to enable me to overcome some of the sins that had been dominating my life. Once I removed myself entirely from the situations, friendships, and relationships I was in, God had room to give me the victory. At times, this is the only solution.

Standards

"He has told you, O man, what is good; and what does the Lord require of you but to do justice, and to love kindness, and to walk humbly with your God?" (Micah 6:8).

Becoming a man of integrity, however, requires submission to God's standards. To do this we must first admit God has standards. Many have watered down God's words to the point that all you have left is a nice book with a few decent platitudes and words of wisdom inside. No, the Gospel is brutally honest with us. It tells us we are fallen and horrible creatures, willing to do all manner of evil.

Quoting from the Old Testament, mostly the Psalms, Paul writes, *"as it is written: 'None is righteous, no, not one; no one understands; no one seeks for God. All have turned aside; together they have become worthless; no one does good, not even one.'"* *"Their throat is an open grave; they use their tongues to deceive."* *"The venom of asps is under their lips."* *"Their mouth is full of curses and bitterness."* *"Their feet are swift to shed blood; in their paths are ruin and misery, and the way of peace they have not known."* *"There is no fear of God before their eyes"* (Romans 3:10–

18). I don't think these words indicate a big grandpappy in the sky who looks down upon everything we do, saying, "Oh, it's all good."

No, we must confess God has standards. He doesn't want you sleeping with your girlfriend. He isn't fine with a little pornography every now and then. He doesn't condone laziness in the form of three-week *Call of Duty* binges. This is all consecration stuff. God rebukes fornication, laziness, theft, deceit, and the like. "*Now we know that the law is good, if one uses it lawfully, understanding this, that the law is not laid down for the just but for the lawless and disobedient, for the ungodly and sinners, for the unholy and profane, for those who strike their fathers and mothers, for murderers, the sexually immoral, men who practice homosexuality, enslavers, liars, perjurers, and whatever else is contrary to sound doctrine, in accordance with the gospel of the glory of the blessed God with which I have been entrusted*" (1 Timothy 1:8–11). God is looking for men who live lives worthy of the Gospel.

This morning I got my day started with a cup of coffee and a little scripture. Reading from the Gospel of Matthew, I found myself in the Crucifixion account. To me, amidst all of the unlawful trials, the beatings, and the mockery, stands what must have been the most horrible moment of Jesus's entire Crucifixion. "*Now from the sixth hour there was darkness over all the land until the ninth hour*" (Matthew 27:45). I don't believe this was a quiet or peaceful darkness. I don't believe this was a restful three hours. I don't believe this was the calm before the storm, I believe this was the storm. I believe this was the moment God "*made him to be sin who knew no sin, so that in him we might become the righteousness of God*" (2 Corinthians 5:21). I don't think the human mind can even begin to imagine the pain of those three hours for Jesus. We can talk about the physical pain of the Crucifixion all we want, and it was an intense pain we will never understand, but I think the physical pain Jesus experienced had nothing on the mental, emotional, and spiritual pain he must have endured becoming sin for us. The atoning work was the bravest thing any man has ever done.

For us to act as if God has no standards at all is an absolute mockery to the cross of Christ. If He has no standard, no manner of life He requires of His men, then why did He have to brutally suffer for us? God is looking for men who will appreciate His sacrifice on the cross, step up, and embrace the standards and desires of His heart.

Law, License, and Liberty

"So speak and so act as those who are to be judged under the law of liberty" (James 2:12).

Maybe this strikes a chord with you, but perhaps with a bit of reservation. After all, you know Christians are not under the law but are under grace. We have a love relationship with God. The law helped you turn to Him because it pronounced you guilty, but you feel it is no longer necessary today because you've already turned to Him. On the one hand, you can appreciate talk of standards, boundaries, or rules, but on the other hand, you are fearful of slipping into legalism. You long deeply to walk and live in the grace of God, knowing it is God's will for you and, frankly, a far better place to live than under the law.

Let me describe four types of believers to you. The first person I would describe is **the legalistic believer**. For this person, rules and regulations are a way to try to feel approved by God. This believer's insecurity before God is evidenced through a performance-based relationship with

Him. This believer receives the wonderful and free gift of the Gospel, only to subsequently attempt to pay Him back. Like a child mowing the grass on December 26 to try to pay for the presents received on December 25, the legalistic believer somehow thinks the favor of God can be earned.

Not only does this person attempt to earn what God has already given, but this believer also attempts to earn God's future favor for his or her life. By producing good works, reading the Bible, or registering impeccable church attendance, this person feels God owes something to whoever does these things. Knowing the Gospel of grace, this kind of believer might never actually confess to believing this, but for all practical purposes, this is the belief inside this person's heart.

The problems with this view and lifestyle are manifold, but two stand out. First, this person has a ridiculously low view of God. His Holiness is not all that high. This God is more akin to the pagan deities who are bound to respond to the lifestyles of men. Instead of worshipping and serving a high, lofty, and invisible God, the legalistic believer serves a sort of genie in the bottle type of god who must repay whoever performs wonderful deeds. Second, this person has a ridiculously high view of self. This pride leads to thinking it is actually possible to earn something from God. This kind of relationship with God is no relationship at all.

The next kind of Christian rejects legalism, instead **turning to license**. Often this is a simple pendulum swing by someone who has experienced a more legalistic approach to God, and who eventually revolts and heads to the other extreme. Tired of living under rules or regulations, this kind of believer takes the free gift of God and runs with it, so to speak. This person is terrified of reform, review, or any standard whatsoever. Being a church person, he or she would likely never confess this fear, but the reality inside this person's heart is a terror of saying no to any sinful craving lest this causes a slip back into legalism.

The problem with this view and lifestyle are many. For one, it really isn't a relationship with God at all. As a husband and father, I have obligations to my wife and children. These obligations don't quench my love relationship with them, but enhance it. Besides, it is difficult to imagine having a relationship with someone as loving, pure, and holy as God without seeing substantial transformation in my own character and lifestyle. Additionally, this is usually just a thinly veiled attempt at continuing to be the lord of my own life, my own little god and rule maker. I get to be the governor and don't have to submit to anything or anyone. We are thankful for a feeling of security concerning our impending death, as in we feel pretty good about going to heaven, but in this life here on earth, we are free to continue on as we please.

A third kind of Christian seeks to **balance out the legalistic and license lifestyles** by resisting either extreme and instead attempts to live right in the middle. The goal of this believer is "to not be too legalistic," but also to avoid "going too far" into liberties. Like Jonny Cash, this person wants to walk the line. This produces a schizophrenic type of believer who bounces wildly between a few rules and regulations and moments of needing to "tap into their wild side." This kind of Christian has a Bible, goes to church, and maybe serves a little bit, but still has to party from time to time or sleep with the person he or she dates in order to keep from being too legalistic.

Finally, there is the believer who has discovered the grace of God to such an incredible degree, this person has **discovered liberty**. Liberty communicates the idea of being set free, and that is exactly what has happened in this believer's life. For this person, it's not about legalism, license, or some kind of juggling act between the two, but an absolute freedom to follow and love God with all of the believer's heart, mind, soul, and strength. This kind of Christian doesn't want to obey God or follow His dictates in order to earn anything from Him, but simply because of a love for Him. This believer longs to be well-pleasing in His sight. His grace has so impacted this person's soul, this kind of believer can't help but live for Him. There is no begrudging obligation in his or her relationship with God, but a healthy brand of thankfulness which leads to a feeling of responsibility toward God.

The words of Paul help us understand this lifestyle. To Titus he writes, *"For the grace of God has appeared, bringing salvation for all people, training us to renounce ungodliness and worldly passions, and to live self-controlled, upright, and godly lives in the present age"* (Titus 2:11–12). In other words, a proper appreciation for the grace of God teaches us we should be done with the old life and live a new life under God's standards. Or, to look at the bookends of Paul's entire paragraph, *"For the grace of God has appeared...to redeem us from all lawlessness and to purify for himself a people for his own possession who are zealous for good works"* (from Titus 2:11–14). In other words, a proper appreciation of the grace of God produces a zeal for the good works of God inside of our lives.

I call this liberty because this person is able to live a truly free kind of life. To be blunt, this person can have sex with whomever he or she wishes, drink as much as wanted, and buy whatever is desired, simply because God has won over this believer's heart and the chief desire of this believer is to please Him. In response to God's wonderful grace, this Christian only wants to enjoy sex with the spouse God gave him, never wants to become intoxicated with any substance, and wants God to direct his spending habits. This is where I long to be.

Best Practices

"Beloved, I urge you as sojourners and exiles to abstain from the passions of the flesh, which wage war against your soul. Keep your conduct among the Gentiles honorable, so that when they speak against you as evildoers, they may see your good deeds and glorify God on the day of visitation" (1 Peter 2:11–12).

Obviously, people are watching our lives. This isn't the chief motivation to love and serve God, but as Peter explained, it is a motivation. The world we live in needs and should see many Christian men who live lives of integrity. Guys who live lives full of grace, good works, and faithfulness. Men who are dependable, trustworthy, and a cut above. Unfortunately, much of what others see of Christian men is hypocrisy and inconsistency, which makes our Christianity less appealing to them. Now, we can bemoan this universally, or we can take care of this individually. Here are some practical areas in which we can live a consecrated life.

Before taking a look at a few of the common temptations men deal and struggle with, I think it would be good to take a quick look at some of the practical ways we can consecrate ourselves before God. God has given us weapons in this war we are in as men, and they are spiritual in nature. As Paul writes, *"For the weapons of our warfare are not of the flesh but have divine power to destroy strongholds"* (2 Corinthians 10:4). What follows is a sturdy list of "best practices" or weapons a Christian man can use.

Devotions

"I rise before dawn and cry for help; I hope in your words" (Psalm 119:147)

Called "devotions" because it is the practice of devoted people, a daily appointment with God is a massive weapon in the Christian man's arsenal. Sometimes referred to as quiet time or Bible study, devotions are often best enjoyed in the morning before the day really begins and are a time when a man is able to pour over scripture and communicate with God in prayer. Again, legalism is not the goal, but a love-based relationship with God. A time like this provides the man of God with an opportunity to hear the voice of God speaking into his life. The encouragement, direction, and strength gained from a time like this are immense.

There are plenty of good Bible reading schedules a man could borrow and implement in his own life, but as stated earlier, a favorite of mine has been the three Old Testament chapters and one New Testament chapter daily, mixed with a Psalm or Proverb of the day. Your style will vary, and clearly there will be seasons you are more diligent than others, but the idea is to press on and make this into a habit. Whatever suits your current taste and season of life, I encourage you to get into a regular practice and discipline of a daily devotional life.

Study

"Do your best to present yourself to God as one approved, a worker who has no need to be ashamed, rightly handling the word of truth" (2 Timothy 2:15).

By the very nature of it, your daily devotional time will have a limited amount of studiousness attached to it. Not that you will take your daily Bible reading lightly, but the relational nature of that time, an unwillingness to bring in endless study helps during that hour, or a more rapid Bible reading pace will keep most men from going incredibly deep in their studies during morning devotions. Still, there is a need in all of us to better learn the word of God. This comes through the study of the Bible.

Hopefully you will attend a church that is willing to teach the Bible. Hearing the Bible taught weekly will greatly benefit your soul. Another way to learn scripture is to join a smaller Bible study or study group. In my home church, various groups gather together weekly to answer homework questions regarding the previous week's sermon, which is taken directly from the Bible. Additionally, you could study the Bible personally by purchasing a few decent commentaries, a Bible dictionary, or a thick study Bible. For me, listening to Bible teaching has been the greatest single tool in helping me understand the word of God. Fortunately, much of this can be done electronically through the use of modern technology.

Reading

"How much better to get wisdom than gold! To get understanding is to be chosen rather than silver" (Proverbs 16:16).

Another great way to consecrate yourself unto God is by reading books by solid Christian authors. Although the Bible effectively touches on a multitude of subjects for our growth, you won't find entire books of the Bible dedicated to manhood, marriage, finances, or parenting. In addition to books on the subjects I just listed, I find that a good Christian biography or a character study on different men or women of the Bible can be incredibly inspiring.

Get into the habit of reading solid Christian books. Two major difficulties come to mind. One is that if you have never been much of a reader, it can be a very difficult habit to learn. It will be difficult for you to turn off the television, shut down your Internet-ready devices, and get into a book. Still, you've made it this far in this book, so at the very least your habit is developing. Perhaps a media fast where you abstain from all forms of media for a month or so could help you learn a new routine. Additionally, you might be helped with an audio book or two to get you going. Also, you might not want to begin by trying to read a thousand-page systematic theology book, but shorter, more manageable books to get you rolling.

A second difficulty lies in the selecting of materials to read. We live in a wonderful information age, but much of that information is unhelpful. With the dawning of Internet bookstore retailers like Amazon, where any book can be sold, came the dusk of bricks and mortar Christian bookstores where books might have been hand-selected for theological soundness and quality. One suggestion would be to find a pastor or a friend whom you admire for their biblical acumen and ask them to point you in the right direction for a book or two. Soon you will be well on your way.

Church

"Not neglecting to meet together, as is the habit of some, but encouraging one another, and all the more as you see the Day drawing near" (Hebrews 10:25).

Being a part of a good church is important to the life of the Christian man. Unfortunately, many men see church as an optional accessory, unimportant to their ambitions and goals. Jesus, however, loves, leads, and died for the church. In His opinion, the church is something worth actively engaging in, instead of merely being a passive member of. That said, let me communicate two things.

For one, the selection of the church is an important process. Although things like an excellent musical experience, an expertly put together children's or youth program, or friendly greeters standing at the front door can be a blessing, they are hardly the most important details in selecting a church. Obviously a safe environment for your children is of utmost importance, and certainly you will want to find a church you think you could eventually fit into, but the most important factor to look for is healthy biblical leadership. Are the pastors men of integrity, and do they teach the word of God? Although these factors won't pop out like a well-groomed lawn or a freshly swept parking lot, they aren't all that impossible to discern, either. Paul told Timothy to *"preach the word"* (2 Timothy 4:2). Find a pastoral team and church willing to do so.

Secondly, it isn't all about simply finding that church. Once you find it, adopt it. Join it. If they have a membership, become a member. Give yourself to it. In whatever ways appropriate in that church setting, let yourself be known. You and the pastor don't need to become BFFs, but introducing yourself to the pastoral team and making some decent friendships in the church is a wonderful place to start. Begin serving and learning what your new church family is like.

Community

"And day by day, attending the temple together and breaking bread in their homes, they received their food with

glad and generous hearts" (Acts 2:46).

Fellowship was a distinguishing mark of the early church. Because they had come to Christ, they were increasingly countercultural. This necessitated new bonds and relationships, a true dependence upon one another. If you are going to live a consecrated life unto God in this world, you're going to need a few Christian friends to help you along in your journey. Let me encourage you to find Christian friendship and community in the church you are in. A good church will have some kind of plan in place in order for its people to engage in more meaningful Christian relationship. Give yourself to it and form the all-important human bonds that are necessary to living the Christian life.

One cannot study the New Testament without observing all of the "one another's" found therein. We are called to *"love one another,"* *"live in harmony with one another,"* and *"bear one another's burdens,"* actions that are not as easily accomplished in the larger congregation on Sunday mornings (John 15:12, Romans 12:16, Galatians 6:2). In response to this realization, some have chosen to shun the larger corporate gatherings, but it would be silly to attempt to cram everything the Christian life is supposed to be into one Sunday meeting. You must have the experience of both, the experience of the large and the small. Gathering publicly and invisibly on Sundays is a wonderful way to honor Christ, while gathering from home to home throughout the week is a great way to develop community and relationship with one another.

Serve

"Whoever would be great among you must be your servant" (Mark 10:43).

Unless we give our lives to a cause greater than ourselves, and unless we pour into the lives of others, we will suffer an inevitable and gradual shift into self-introspection, selfishness, and ultimately despair. Jesus came to serve, and He is our model for life. Later I will talk about our service toward people within our families and everyday lives, but here I mean to emphasize the service inside of your local church and in your community.

It is commonly said that 10 percent of the people do 90 percent of the work in a local church setting. To me, these numbers could be interpreted a few different ways. For example, maybe numbers like this indicate that a church might be trying to do too much or are trying to scratch a non-existent itch. Still, it is true that many people never discover the joy of serving in their local congregation. Volunteer. Serve. Sign up. You will find great joy and reward in it. Plus chicks dig it.

Additionally, it is good to serve your community somehow in some way. Whether through acts of generosity, such as giving to foster children or supporting single mothers, or through acts of mercy where you are actually serving with boots on the ground, deep blessing is found when serving our world. Remember, *"religion that is pure and undefiled before God, the Father, is this: to visit orphans and widows in their affliction, and to keep oneself unstained from the world"* (James 1:27). Perhaps you need to go on missions trips to Third World countries or bring meals to a battered women's shelter, but reaching your world in this way is vital to your consecration.

Stand Strong

"And if it is evil in your eyes to serve the Lord, choose this day whom you will serve, whether the gods your fathers

served in the region beyond the River, or the gods of the Amorites in whose land you dwell. But as for me and my house, we will serve the Lord" (Joshua 24:15).

In the following chapter, we will begin to look at general temptation, followed by specific temptations men deal with. But here, as we've looked at our consecration, I would encourage you to choose to serve the Lord. Perhaps this is an initial decision for you. Perhaps all of this is brand-spanking new. Or, perhaps like me, these words stand as a simple encouragement to continue and press on, taking your walk with God more seriously than ever.

Paul the apostle told us to, *"Be watchful, stand firm in the faith, act like men, be strong"* (1 Corinthians 16:13). What an incredible exhortation. First of all, be watchful. Be on guard. Understand that there is an enemy who seeks to disqualify you and render you useless to the kingdom of God. Secondly, stand firm in the faith. Don't be a flimsy, unstable man, but a man with backbone and integrity. Thirdly, Paul writes, act like men. The differences between boys and men are obvious. Boys pretend to go to war, while men actually go. Men take responsibility, just like the ultimate man, Jesus Christ, took responsibility for us. And finally, be strong. Infused with the power and strength of the Spirit of God, stand up and fight for your own life and the lives of those you love. Be a consecrated man. For all of eternity, you will not regret it.

Chapter 5: Your Life

"Or do you not know that your body is a temple of the Holy Spirit within you, whom you have from God? You are not your own, for you were bought with a price. So glorify God in your body" (1 Corinthians 6:19–20).

As Christian men, we are under new management. We have been purchased by the precious blood of Jesus Christ, so our lives are no longer our own. We are now to make ourselves slaves of righteousness and slaves of God (Romans 6:18, 22). Because of our new connection to the living God and a living organism He established called the church, we are responsible to others for our lives and actions. We are no longer islands to the world around us. We are called to live a new brand of life. In one sense, you should dispense immediately with the idea that this is *your* life, because it isn't. It now belongs to God. Fortunately for us, however, this new life God has called us to live is the best brand of life available.

In another sense, this life is incredibly and most definitely yours. In other words, the flavor, tenor, and focus of your life are truly up to you. Paul, in speaking of his work in the Corinthian church, said this: *"Now if anyone builds on the foundation with gold, silver, precious stones, wood, hay, straw—each one's work will become manifest, for the Day will disclose it, because it will be revealed by fire, and <u>the fire will test what sort of work each one has done</u>. If the work that anyone has built on the foundation survives, he will receive a reward. If anyone's work is burned up, he will suffer loss, though he himself will be saved, but only as through fire"* (1 Corinthians 3:12–15).

Paul was intensely interested in living a life that would

endure. He wanted his works to be of the gold, silver, and precious stones variety, the kind that can pass through the fires of eternal judgment. Paul wasn't confused; he didn't think for a moment he could earn his salvation. Instead, Paul understood the principle of eternal reward. Rather than live an eternally meaningless existence by producing works that were tantamount to wood, hay, and stubble, all perishable within the fire, Paul wanted his life to count for something, to count for eternity.

Make no mistake, this is a war. There are wicked elements at play designed to keep you from living this eternally valuable life. I referenced it earlier, but one major hindrance to living this lifestyle is the world system that wars against our souls. Like gravity, the world pulls against everything we do. Additionally, there is an invisible enemy called the devil who controls a powerful and real army of demonic forces: *"for we do not wrestle against flesh and blood, but against the rulers, against the authorities, against the cosmic powers over this present darkness, against the spiritual forces of evil in the heavenly places"* (Ephesians 6:12). On top of all this is the absolute weakness of our own flesh, bodies that have already enjoyed the pleasures of sin. We may be new creatures in Christ Jesus, but these bodies of ours have tasted sin. Since the world, devil, and flesh are very real, the Christian man can anticipate getting kicked in the groin by temptation.

Temptation

"But each person is tempted when he is lured and enticed by his own desire. Then desire when it has conceived gives birth to sin, and sin when it is fully grown brings forth death" (James 1:14–15).

Temptation is a tool designed to drop the man of God into sinful practices. The strategy is to lure and entice people away from God by their own desires embedded within them. The first result of temptation is simply sin, but the end game and goal of temptation is to bring us to a place called death (see James 1:14–15). This strategy of Satan is brutal yet consistent.

Note the strategy Satan employed at the first temptation (Genesis 3). His first tactic was to get the woman to doubt the plan and will of God. Satan said to the woman, *"Did God actually say, 'You shall not eat of any tree in the garden'?"* (Genesis 3:1). He wanted to put the woman off balance by getting her to doubt God's true meaning when He commanded them not to eat of the tree of the knowledge of good and evil. This same doubt is embedded in the minds of modern Christians when they wonder things like, "did God really forbid premarital sex?" "Is it really that bad for me to cheat on my taxes?" Or "certainly God wants me to land a great job, so he won't mind if I lie on my resume, right?"

Another original and brutal tactic of Satan is to put God's commands in a negative light. The Garden of Eden was actually a very permissive place. Even by modern standards, I don't think any of us would refer to it as restrictive. They were allowed to eat of any tree in the entire garden, with only one exception. Satan, however, when asking about the command of God, flipped it to sound like a negative. Again, *"Did God actually say, 'You shall not eat of any tree in the garden'?"* (Genesis 3:1).

When the man of God experiences temptation, the only thing he will be able to see is that which has been forbidden, rather than the immense blessings that come from his freedom in Christ Jesus. Don't expect Satan to highlight the wonderful joy you receive from living inside God's parameters. He's a snake and a liar, so he will never remind you of that truth. He won't do that. Instead, it is up to you to bring *"every thought into captivity to the obedience of Christ"* (2 Corinthians 10:5 NKJV).

In her response, Eve gave in to a touch of legalism when she said, *"We may eat the fruit of the trees of the garden; but of the fruit of the tree which is in the midst of the garden, God has said, 'You shall not eat it, nor shall you touch it, lest you die"* (Genesis 3:2–3). Notice her little addition to God's command. God had told them not to eat of the tree of the knowledge of good and evil, but she declared God had also told them not to touch it. No eating, but also no touching! I believe this little insertion is evidence of the battle that was waging inside of her heart at that very moment. Did she believe God was good or did she believe God was a tyrant? Was He a restrictive God, a cosmic kill-joy?

When temptation happens today, the same questions will be asked. Alternately, when we give into temptation, it's as if we are saying what God has provided for us is not the best, but He has withheld from us. We see Him in a negative light, whether we say it or not, and we choose against Him. Again, these thoughts must be taken captive.

Satan went on to say, *"You will not surely die"* (Genesis 3:4). This is the blatant lie embedded in all temptation—the idea that our sin is not that bad, that it won't lead to the consequences promised us in God's word. We think no one will see. We believe our sin only affects us and no one else. Blinded by temptation, we doubt the consequences of sin. If only Adam and Eve could have seen clearly beyond this moment of temptation. If only they could have seen the generations of death, the murder of their own son, and, ultimately, the death of God's Son that would occur as a result of their actions.

Our sin won't result in the same brand of horrible

consequences as Adam and Eve's, but our sin can and will negatively impact large groups and future generations of people. This becomes painfully obvious when imagining a world without even just sexual sin. Families would be stronger. Children would have greater mental health. Populations would be free of various diseases. Spending might decrease as seductive advertising lost its power. Men and women would be more secure in themselves, eliminating many of the issues caused by our insecurities. The imagination could run wild with hypotheticals, but suffice it to say, the world would be a gladder place if even just one sin were eliminated, because sin produces death.

Oh, for us to see the consequences of our actions! Think about the people in your own life. How many times have you talked to a man or a woman whose life has obviously been impacted, perhaps even for multiple generations, because of the "forbidden fruit" someone in their lives decided to eat?

"For God knows that in the day you eat of it your eyes will be opened, and you will be like God, knowing good and evil" (Genesis 3:5). Satan continued his barrage. He told the woman what she would be like on the day she ate of that fruit. She would know good and evil. At that point in human history, God had been the only one to declare something good. On the different days of creation, God saw that what He had made was good (Genesis 1:4, 10, 12, 18, 21, 25). After creating man, at the conclusion of it all, *"God saw everything that he had made, and indeed it was very good. So the evening and the morning were the sixth day"* (Genesis 1:31). But Satan continued to pepper the woman's heart and mind. *"You, and no longer God, need to decide what is good and what is evil,"* Satan whispered into her ear.

"So when the woman saw that the tree was good for food, that it was pleasant to the eyes, and a tree desirable to make one wise, she took of its fruit and ate. She also

gave to her husband with her, and he ate" (Genesis 3:6). For the first time, a human being decided what was good and what was evil. Eve saw the fruit and decided it was good for food. In other words, the first time human hearts decided what was right and what was wrong, there was cataclysmic disaster.

Ultimately then, temptation boils down to a lordship issue. Do we believe we know better than God? Is there a sense within our hearts that we know what is good while He does not? Will we allow Him to be lord? When temptation comes along, it is good for us to remember our loving, heavenly Father. It is good to remember that He always knows best, that He loves us and would never withhold His blessings from us. If He has labeled something as off limits, it is merely for our own blessing. Even if it looks good in our own human eyes, it must be resisted because He has decided it is damaging and injurious, "not good." Remember, sin is not bad because it's forbidden, but forbidden because it is bad.

Satan wants to take you out, hard and fast. He isn't interested in you or your life. His only interest is to destroy your life. The lake of fire has been built for him and his demons, and he lives to take as many people there as possible (Matthew 25:41). Whatever he has to do to violently destroy you he will do without mercy. He came as a snake in the beginning and has operated as a snake ever since. Temptation is a tool in his pocket, a tool designed to produce death, to kill. He has been a killer from the beginning and he is gunning for us, gentlemen.

Areas of Temptation

"For all that is in the world—the lust of the flesh, the lust of the eyes, and the pride of life—is not of the Father but is of the world" (1 John 2:16).

Notice, however, the three specific areas Eve was tempted in. She *"saw that the tree was good for food, that it was pleasant to the eyes, and a tree desirable to make one wise"* (Genesis 3:6). First, this temptation appealed to her **bodily appetites** because she saw it was good for food. In the New Testament, John refers to this as the "lust of the flesh" (1 John 2:16). Today this version of temptation can be found in things like fornication, gluttony, and substance abuse. Additionally, this temptation appealed to her **eyesight** as the tree appeared "pleasant to the eyes." John refers to this as the "lust of the eyes." This temptation is manifested today in sins like covetousness, gambling, and jealousy. Finally, Eve was filled with **pride** as she found the tree "desirable to make one wise." John calls this the "pride of life," a sin evidenced by rap star boasters, fame-chasers, and power-mongers. Satan attacks in all three areas today. His playbook is incredibly small, but incredibly effective.

The Lie of Temptation

Another brutal lie that occurs during temptation is the idea that you are the only one experiencing such temptation. When temptation hits we can feel alone, twisted, or perverted. The reality, however, is that *"No temptation has overtaken you except such as is common to man; but God is faithful, who will not allow you to be tempted beyond what you are able, but with the temptation will also make the way of escape, that you may be able to bear it"* (1 Corinthians 10:13).

The good news is twofold. First, we are not alone in our struggle against temptation. Other men are in the fight as well. This doesn't mean we are all tempted with the exact same things or to the same degree, but every temptation has a similar route. It is important to understand the wicked capability inside all of us. Secondly, it is wonderful to discover that God has provided a built-in way of escape with every temptation. There is no temptation so monumental that we must engage in it. No, God will always provide a route for the man of God to take.

Joseph is a wonderful example of this kind of man. As a young man far from home, his master's wife began to lust for him. She persistently attempted to get Joseph to fornicate with her, offering him her body on a continual basis. Even though his family and friends were far away, Joseph wouldn't budge. One day he was alone in the house and this woman thought she had her opportunity. She grabbed Joseph by the garment and said, "Lie with me" (Genesis 39:12). At that moment there wasn't even room for conversation. Joseph wiggled out of his jacket and simply ran out of that house, making himself a wonderful example to generations of men who have admired him for his courageous retreat.

Understand that temptation is an absolute beast. We are truly up against it. The world, like the devil, is incredibly strong, but our flesh doesn't help matters at all because it is incredibly susceptible to temptation. However, we serve a God much stronger than the world, the devil, or our sinful desires that rage inside us. His Spirit within us is able to overcome the inadequacies of our flesh. "*I say then: Walk in the Spirit, and you shall not fulfill the lust of the flesh*" (Galatians 5:16). Don't think of God as a weakling who cannot overcome something as strong as temptation. He created the universe by speaking it into existence, so He can also help us keep our pants on.

Sexual Purity

"Marriage is honorable among all, and the bed undefiled;

but fornicators and adulterers God will judge" (Hebrews 13:4).

No book aimed at disciplining Christian men would be complete without dealing with the subject of sexual purity. From Lamech, the first polygamist found in Genesis 4, to the Ephesian mob chanting to their sex god in Acts 19, and everywhere in between, God has always warned his people against sexual immorality. There were moments in Israel's history where sexual sin would cripple their entire nation, just as there are moments today when a pastor's sexual escapades can cripple an entire church.

As stated earlier, it is important to recognize God has standards in areas like our sexuality. To put it rather simply and succinctly, fornication is when you engage in sexual activity before marriage, while adultery is when you engage in sexual activity outside of marriage. The psychological trauma done to children, sexually transmitted diseases, broken homes, unwanted pregnancies, sexual addictions, and the like should be evidence enough that all forms of sex outside of marriage were never God's intention. Instead, Satan took a wonderful and powerful act, a very fun gift from God, and promoted it as something enjoyable outside of marriage. And, obviously, the act itself can be enjoyable, albeit with sometimes disastrous consequences.

I long to see a day when godly men refuse to engage in sexual activity until they are married. Unfortunately, the myth of the necessity of cohabitation in order to figure out if marriage is right for you has permeated this culture. It is getting rarer and rarer to find young couples willing to wait to be married before engaging each other sexually. If you are a single man reading this book, I implore you to do yourself, your future wife, and your future family a favor and abstain from sexual immorality. I know sexual sin is found quite often among married men as well, but I need to plead with the single men in the church. Stand strong. Every one of your friends might be sleeping with their girlfriends, imbibing porn, or chasing sex all over town, but you have got to be different. Endure. It is so worth it if you do.

Abstaining From Sexual Immorality

"For this is the will of God, your sanctification: that you should abstain from sexual immorality" (1 Thessalonians 4:3).

Now, when it comes to avoiding sexual immorality, Paul gives us some wonderful instruction in 1 Thessalonians 4. To me, this is a wonderful place for us to turn, because the Thessalonian culture was an incredibly sexually immoral culture, much like ours. It is a culture we can relate to much more easily than the biblical Jewish culture with its embedded morals and respect for the law of God. No, the Thessalonian culture was rooted in Greco-Roman thinking. They had it all: fornication, adultery, homosexuality, pedophilia, and more pornographic and erotic perversions and practices than I care to name. On top of all that, they had mystery religions which came prepackaged with prostitution as a part of their worship services.

We also live in an increasingly sexually immoral culture. This culture believes that man is basically good, so only the most heinous activities should not be tolerated, meaning you basically have to be a modern day Hitler to qualify for the wrath of God, while the rest of us are just pretty good people who mess up from time to time. This, combined with the belief that sex is merely a biological function, means our culture believes we should be controlled by our urges, not our morals. To them, anything consensual goes, so casual sex will pervade. Because sex is worshipped so highly, any potential mate must be tested for sexual compatibility before anything close to a marriage commitment is made.

The first thing we must discover as Christian men is that God is interested in our sexual purity. Have you ever wanted to know the will of God for your life? Well, Paul states clearly that the will of God is our sanctification and that we should abstain from sexual immorality (1 Thessalonians 4:3). God isn't nosy or overstepping His bounds, but is a loving Father who longs for us to experience the very best. Know that God is concerned with your sexual activity.

How—Three Ways

Paul then tells the Thessalonians how to avoid sexual immorality in three distinct ways. Here's the first one: "*that each of you should know how to possess his own vessel in sanctification and honor*" (1 Thessalonians 4:4). The first step a Jesus guy needs to take in avoiding sexual immorality is to **get control of his own body**. Before we were in Christ, we were ruled and dominated by our passions. Now, however, we are told to know how to control our own bodies.

This first step is genius because the common myth is that men cannot help themselves, and they cannot control their own bodies. Men commonly believe their actions are subservient to the desires, tastes, and passions of their body. The Corinthians used this same argument with Paul. They told Paul that just as food was meant for the stomach and the stomach was meant for food, so was sexual activity meant for the body and the body was meant for sexual activity. They used this logic to explain why they had no control over themselves. But Paul corrected their faulty logic when he said, "*Now the body is not for sexual immorality but for the Lord, and the Lord for the body*" (1 Corinthians 6:13). In other words, while it might be true that a stomach finds its highest fulfillment with food, the body does not find its highest fulfillment with sex. The body was made for God and finds its highest fulfillment in and with God. By getting into the word of God and walking in the Spirit of God we will be able to, more and more, gain control over our bodies.

In his next insight on how to avoid sexual immorality, Paul tells the Thessalonians to live "*not in passion of lust, like the Gentiles who do not know God*" (1 Thessalonians 4:5). In other words, the believing man must understand he is called to **live a countercultural life**. This expectation is important to the success of living a sexually pure life. You absolutely cannot expect the culture to hold the same biblical values you are going to hold when it comes to sexuality. Your standards and lifestyle will be different. You have to expect to be mocked, scoffed at, and ridiculed. You have to be prepared for funny conversations and odd looks. Why don't you sleep with your girlfriend? Why don't you want to look at this porn? Why don't you entertain the thought of an affair? The reality is that you are different.

And you definitely are different. "*Beloved, I beg you as sojourners and pilgrims, abstain from fleshly lusts which war against the soul*" (1 Peter 2:11). According to Peter we are pilgrims and sojourners; we don't belong here. This world is not our home. When Jesus offered up His body on the cross for our redemption, His full intention was to bring many sons to glory (Hebrews 2:10). He has gone to prepare a place for us and will one day return to take us to our eternal home, a home far greater and more significant than our home on earth (John 14:2-3). If, like Abraham, you are longing for that future city whose designer and builder is God, then you will expect to live a countercultural life (Hebrews 11:10).

Finally, Paul instructs the Thessalonians "*that no one*

should take advantage of and defraud his brother in this matter" (1 Thessalonians 4:6). This is one of the more interesting steps Paul delivers to the Thessalonians on how to free yourself from sexual immorality. Basically, Paul tells them to consider how their sexual sin is going to affect others. In other words, the believing man should **consider others over himself** when it comes to his sexual activity.

This applies in three distinct ways. First of all, the word "brother" could simply indicate **mankind**. So, Paul is telling us that our sexual impurity actually negatively impacts humanity in some way. It might seem like a drop in the bucket to us, but we are actually polluting said bucket with our sexual immorality. Second, we must also consider how our sexual sin affects **our family in Christ**. The church is defrauded when individuals inside of the church live outside of the boundaries God has given us sexually. None of us would want to be guilty of taking the members of Christ and making them members of a harlot (see 1 Corinthians 6:15). Finally, we must consider how our sexual sin affects **those closest to us**. Our children, both present and future, will be negatively affected by our sexual sin. Obviously, our wives or future wives will also be hurt through our sexual sin. This applies even if they were the girlfriend or fiancé we fornicated with before marriage. Either way, it is hurtful sin that must be dealt with.

I know many good, married Christian men who, after being convicted of their sexual sin with their fiancés before marriage, decided they needed to deal with their sin by apologizing to their wives for that past sin and lack of leadership. Many of them have taken it a step further by confessing their sin to other brothers in Christ and pastors or elders. The refreshment that comes from true repentance is life-giving (Acts 3:19). These men are heroes to me.

Why?

As Paul continues his instruction to the Thessalonians, he moves on into the motive for sexual purity. To get control of our bodies, learn to live counter culturally, and consider how our sin affects others is the how. But why? What is my real motivation? Again, Paul explains this in three distinct ways.

First, "*because the Lord is the avenger of all such, as we also forewarned you and testified*" (1 Thessalonians 4:6). In other words, one great motive for sexual purity is the **vengeance of God**. God is a just judge, and it is His responsibility and duty to discipline for sin. Not only that, but He has promised to build in consequences for sexual immorality. Damaged marriages, broken families, divorce, disease, absence of the blessing of God, lost eternal rewards, and even death are some of the consequences attached to this sin.

Secondly, **this is not our calling**: "*For God did not call us to uncleanness, but in holiness*" (1 Thessalonians 4:7). God has a higher and better calling for us. Why avoid sexual sin? Because God has called us to a more honorable and exalted type of life. He's called us to something much better: "*I, therefore, the prisoner of the Lord, beseech you to walk worthy of the calling with which you were called*" (Ephesians 4:1). We are not powerless creatures left to follow the impulses of our bodies like animals, but are instead called to be figureheads for justice, patriarchs of godly generations, and leaders of people.

Finally, we don't engage in sexual immorality because of **God's Spirit within us**: "*Therefore he who rejects this does not reject man, but God, who has also given us his Holy Spirit*" (1 Thessalonians 4:8). God has put His Spirit within us, which means He has also put His law into our minds and written it upon our hearts. He is our God and we are His people. Our identity has been so changed by our interaction with God in the Gospel, that it no longer makes sense to live the lifestyle wired to engage in sexual immorality.

Help!

Much of this book is designed to help you when it comes to the temptation toward sexual immorality. Your prayer life, for instance, which we touched on earlier, will provide you with great spiritual strength in the face of lust. Likewise, learning how to be a student of scripture will equip you with one of the greatest weapons of all to combat the fiery darts of the wicked one. Being a part of a healthy church, serving, and getting into a solid community of believers will all work wonders for your sexual integrity.

When it comes to this particular sin, however, it is important to put on a full-on frontal attack. Right after explaining that looking at a woman with lust in your heart is actually tantamount to adultery in the sight of God, Jesus said, "*If your right eye causes you to sin, pluck it out and cast it from you; for it is more profitable for you that one of your members perish, than for your whole body to be cast into hell. And if your right hand causes you to sin, cut it off and cast it from you; for it is more profitable for you that one of your members perish, than for your whole body to be cast into hell*" (Matthew 5:29–30). In other words, be ridiculously aggressive in avoiding this sin. Disable the Internet. Discover an accountability group. Throw away your smart phone. Tell others. Whatever you have to do, do it.

My house is located at the base of a small mountain. The forest on this mountain has been undeveloped and unhindered, so it has grown quite thick. During the winter months, because of the forest growth, the sunlight never gets to my backyard, which means all kinds of weird things grow in my backyard in the winter. During the summer months, however, the sun hits that ground once again, and strange growths cease. This is similar to our lives. When we walk in the darkness, strange growths occur. Bad things happen. Instead, get in the light. Be honest. Get help. Expose your temptations and struggles and watch the power of God come flooding in.

Money

If I taught about money as often as Jesus did, after a while I don't think I would have anyone to preach to. Jesus spent a great deal of His teaching time dealing with this subject. The Bible gives much attention to physical possessions and wealth. Like sexuality, how a man handles His finances is another major consideration of scripture.

An Instrument

One of the first things to understand about finances from a biblical perspective is that money is neither good nor evil, but neutral. In the Bible, money is used to purchase land, food, and merchandise—benign articles—but it is also used to purchase prostitutes and slaves while feeding the greed of men. Contrary to the teachings and ideologies of some, money is not intrinsically wicked. Additionally, contrary to the ideas of others, money is not a god to be worshipped. In other words, money is neutral, while the men who hold the money are not.

We are able to use our money to express our faith, for example. "*Pure and undefiled religion before God and the Father is this: to visit orphans and widows in their trouble, and to keep oneself unspotted from the world*" (James

1:27). To take care of a brother who is in need of worldly goods is one way we can lay down our lives for others as Christ did for us (1 John 3:16–17). Our finances can also be used to fund ministry by sending out workers, supporting existing Gospel ministers, and taking care of the poor (Acts 13:1–3, 18:1–4, 1 Corinthians 9:14, Philippians 4:14–19, Galatians 2:9–10). A simple reading of the book of Acts ought to explain all of this quite nicely.

Obviously, the aggressive expansion of the Gospel took a bit of financial commitment on the part of the church. The sending out of Paul and Barnabas, the support of Paul in various cities, and the supply given to Paul when he was under house arrest enabled churches to be planted, leaders to be developed, and scripture to be written. Additionally, various churches gave a generous gift to the church in Judea, which was suffering mightily under persecution and financial trial.

Obviously, financial investment goes hand-in-hand with a heart commitment to the kingdom and work of God here on earth. If a man cares little for God's kingdom, he will care little about giving toward God's kingdom. This is why *"the Lord has commanded that those who preach the gospel should live from the gospel"* (1 Corinthians 9:14). Money is an instrument that can be used for good or evil.

Where Is Your Treasure?

Jesus referred to greed as an eye-darkening sin (Matthew 6:22–23). The reason for this is simple: we often don't know when we are acting greedily. If you commit adultery, you know it. If you lie, you know it. But when it comes to greed, we can always find someone who has more than we do, *much* more than we do. Because we can find people who are "more guilty" than us, it is easy to dismiss the sin of greed altogether. I can talk about lust all day long and someone will listen to me, but when I start talking about greed, the audience thins out rather quickly. Rarely does a man think he is guilty of this sin, but money greatly influences our hearts.

Before explaining the eye-darkening nature of greed, Jesus clarified that wherever we put our treasure, there our heart will be also (Matthew 6:21). This is entirely backward to our modern thinking. One would think that whatever they value is naturally where they would put their treasure, meaning their time and, especially, their money. However, Jesus said it was the other way around. Whatever you invest in with your time and your treasure, that is what your heart will eventually be interested in and about. In other words, you will treasure whatever you end up putting your resources into.

In the seventh grade, I took a basic economics class where we selected various stocks to invest in for the duration of the class. Although no real money was exchanged and the investment was completely imaginary, I woke up every day wondering how my Hershey's stock was performing. I had never been interested in the Dow Jones previously, but during that class I routinely checked in with my stock before getting to the baseball scores I was curious about.

This is the principle Jesus taught (Matthews 6:21). Put your treasure somewhere, and your heart will follow your treasure there. I didn't care about the success of the Hershey Company before. As long as they continued making chocolate, I was good. After investing in them, however, my heart changed. When you put your treasure into the kingdom of God, you will become a person who is interested in the things of God.

This is important for us to understand when it comes to

using our money well. It is important for us to put it in the right places, so our hearts will grow in the right way. We want to treasure the things Jesus treasures. We want our priorities to be straight. The easiest way to determine where the priorities of our heart are really going to lie is by looking at how we spend our money.

There are various heart attitudes concerning money that are sinful, four of which I will mention here. The first and most obvious is covetousness, which leads to all kinds of sin. Paul said it best when he wrote, *"For the love of money is a root of all kinds of evil"* (1 Timothy 6:10). Entire reprehensible industries, like the sex trade or pornography, wouldn't exist without a deep love for money. A sinful desire for money causes people to compromise their morals.

Another error is the feeling of superiority that can come with riches: *"Command those who are rich in this present age not to be haughty"* (1 Timothy 6:17). Human nature is simple. We believe the more, the better. But for those of us in the church, no matter how much we have, we are on equal ground with all of our brothers and sisters in Christ.

Additionally, there is also the sinful and false sense of security that can come from money: *"nor to trust in uncertain riches but in the living God"* (1 Timothy 6:17). This is a major area of deception. We often believe that if we have enough in the bank account, then we are secure. But, like tomorrow, riches are uncertain. It is far better to trust in the living God at all times, no matter how much you have built up in your 401(k).

Finally, there is the sin of feeling significant as a result of your money (Ecclesiastes 5:10). But to find your confidence in what you possess is pure vanity, not to mention incredibly empty. You will still be insecure and unstable, because only a solid relationship with God can give you the security and significance you are looking for.

God's Possession

At this point I should communicate the reality that the money in our hands is not actually ours at all. The whole earth and everything in it belongs to God (Psalm 24:1). Everything was created through Him and for Him (Colossians 1:16). We are simply stewards God has entrusted with a certain amount of resources. Just as God gave dominion to man over the earth, to keep and tend it, so God has committed into our trust a certain amount of goods to tend and to keep. Yes, we are to work hard, use our ingenuity, and diligently earn a living. Still, it is good for us to see all that we earn as a gift from God, something that truly belongs to Him. We are merely to steward it well.

This principle should impact how every one of Jesus's men spends and lives in the financial realm. To see ourselves as stewards of money that belongs to God will impact our financial priorities. Instead of frivolously spending, we will consider each purchase and inquire of God as to the wisdom and necessity of such a purchase. Instead of rushing headlong into further indebtedness, we will carefully run our lives in such a way that debt is not growing, but shrinking. Instead of always spending on our favorite hobby or activity—neutral things money can definitely be useful for—we will be sure to tuck some away for the kingdom of God by investing in our local church, along with church planting efforts, parachurch organizations, or foreign missions.

Planning and Saving

"A good man leaves an inheritance to his children's children, but the sinner's wealth is laid up for the righteous" (Proverbs 13:22).

One highly effective way to be a good steward of the money God has entrusted to you is to set a budget for yourself. Obviously, this is not a new idea, but it is incredibly important to tell your money where it is going to go before you spend it. Too many Christians are wallowing in impossible debt, discovering the truth *"the rich rules over the poor, and the borrower is servant to the lender"* (Proverbs 22:7). It is foolish to go into debt over things that will be worth little once you actually pay them off, like a sweet new television or sports car. When it comes to this kind of debt, in one sense you are spending what isn't yours, sinfully testing God.

The Christian book market is filled with great resources to help you learn how to budget, plan, and get out of debt. I personally love the *Total Money Makeover* by Dave Ramsey, but also currently use Crown's Mvelopes online budgeting service for my family. Whatever resource you use, it is important to make a plan, communicate your plan to others, pray over your plan, and stick with your plan.

In my home, Christina and I establish a budget each year, reviewing our saving and giving goals, but then follow it up with a monthly meeting in order to adjust our budget to reflect the coming month. This can be done as a family or individually.

Inside of your budget, you should have a plan for saving. The idea here is not to hoard and give yourself a false sense of security, but to be a faithful steward of what God has entrusted to your care. As a married man with three daughters, I try to save in specific areas, have an emergency fund for a rainy day, have a life insurance policy in case I am no longer around to provide for my family, and have a health insurance policy that will cover any major medical expense that could financially derail our family.

The place of life you are in and the personal conviction of

your heart might mean you have far less than this, but it also might mean you have far more than this. I know men who have incredibly detailed financial plans in place and are doing a wonderful job providing for their families, while I know others who would consider it a sin to store up too much for themselves, as they feel a strong conviction to give as much as they can. The key is to prayerfully seek God as you make a plan that honors Him by providing for your family and investing in His kingdom, stick to the plan, and revisit it with God and your spouse, if you have one, from time to time.

Generosity

"The wicked borrows but does not pay back, but the righteous is generous and gives" (Psalm 37:21).

The Christian man should have a goal of generosity with, and in, his finances. As Jesus said, it is truly more blessed to give than to receive (Acts 20:35). This isn't a cute maxim, but reality. In another place Jesus said, *"give, and it will be given to you. Good measure, pressed down, shaken together, running over, will be put into your lap. For with the measure you use it will be measured back to you"* (Luke 6:38). In other words, there is a wonderful blessing in store for the man who is willing to be generous with his finances.

Practically speaking, each man must make a determination and a plan on how and when he will give. *"Each one must give as he has decided in his heart"* (2 Corinthians 9:7). If your plan for giving is haphazard and reactive, you likely won't have much to give when the time comes. It is far better to methodically store up and make a plan for your giving.

Paul gives a wonderful explanation of a healthy plan for

giving in 1 Corinthians 16:1-4. "*Now concerning the collection for the saints: as I directed the churches of Galatia, so you also are to do. On the first day of every week, each of you is to put something aside and store it up, as he may prosper, so that there will be no collecting when I come. And when I arrive, I will send those whom you accredit by letter to carry your gift to Jerusalem. If it seems advisable that I should go also, they will accompany me*" (1 Corinthians 16:1–4). Paul directed all the churches in his day to approach their giving in this way.

First of all, this was a weekly experience which occurred on Sundays for them. This was more than a one-time gift. This was an ongoing responsibility and duty. I find that simple line items in my personal budget enable me to accomplish this most easily. By deciding ahead of time how I will give toward my church, missionaries, ministries, and acts of generosity, I am creating a plan and stewarding God's money well.

Secondly, they were personally and individually called to this as Paul addressed "each one" of them. Each man was to take responsibility for his home and finances, finding a way to give. It is easy to think someone else will take care of it. As a local church pastor, I can tell you that major contributions from significant donors can indeed be a blessing, but they cannot begin to scratch the surface on what the planned, consistent, and regular giving of the body of Christ amounts to. Don't leave this job for someone else.

Next, Paul told them to plan for this giving by setting aside and storing up as they earned. For them, this was a weekly experience. Perhaps you are paid monthly or biweekly. Perhaps your major windfall comes once per year. Whatever your situation, as you earn, it is good to set aside for giving and generosity.

Additionally, Paul recognized their giving would be

proportional to their income when he told them to store up "*as he may prosper.*" Although a tithe of ten percent might be a great place for Christians to start in their giving, the goal of the New Testament is to be as generous as possible. One man might only be able to afford to give one dollar out of every ten, while another might be able to afford giving nine dollars out of every ten without skipping a beat.

Finally, Paul expected their giving to be done voluntarily, as he was not willing to pressure them by taking a collection personally. You never would have caught Paul on TV begging for money. If "the ministry cannot go on without your support," perhaps God wants to shut that ministry down. It was important to Paul for their giving to be willing, generous, and cheerful (2 Corinthians 9:5-7). He would not pressure them one bit. Although it will test his faith at times, a Gospel-centered man will love to give.

Tithing?

If you have been around Christians for any length of time, you have probably heard someone ask about the tithe, the giving of ten percent of our income to God. Concerning the Pharisees, religious leaders who had faithfully tithed without caring at all about mercy or justice, Jesus said, "*These you ought to have done* (tithe)*, without neglecting the others* (justice, mercy, and faithfulness)" (Matthew 23:23). Others point to the law being fulfilled in Christ. After all, Jesus took care of it "*by canceling the record of debt that stood against us with its legal demands. This he set aside, nailing it to the cross*" (Colossians 2:14). On the other hand, some would point out that Abraham offered a tithe to Melchizedek way before the law was given, and Jesus is a priest according to the order of Melchizedek according to Hebrews 11, so maybe the tithe is pre-law and still biblical today. Then some will point out that Israel actually gave much more than ten percent to God.

However, wondering if the tithe is for today is probably the wrong question. The better question is this: if everything belongs to God, and if I am to purposefully give, how would God have me to do it? In other words, the New Testament doesn't seem to get into a big debate over the biblical nature of the tithe for the modern church. Instead, the assumption is that a people who have been rocked by the Gospel will desire to be as giving as they possibly can, while still maintaining their responsibilities to their own families.

Sometimes a simple, direct question helps resolve the issue. As a father with three young children in my house right now, I often find myself serving as a referee of sorts. As much as we urge our children to work arguments out between themselves, there are moments where mom or dad must step in. Often, as I listen to the excellent cases presented to me by each child, I grow confused. I have found one simple question very effective. I will often look one of my daughters in the eye and ask, "Have you been as kind as possible to your sister?" She usually knows the answer. Likewise, a question we could ask is, "Have I been as generous as possible?" When questions concerning our generosity and giving and kindness leave the realm of lawful duty and enter into unbridled generosity, we have become more like our Lord who lavishly gave to His people.

General Encouragement

"One gives freely, yet grows all the richer; another withholds what he should give, and only suffers want" (Proverbs 11:24).

You can do this. Some of you, while reading this last

section on finances, have grown slightly uncomfortable. This brand of generosity seems a tall order. None of us is as generous as Christ. We all fail in many ways, but let me encourage you for a moment. By the grace of God and the power of His Holy Spirit, we are able to become like our Lord by being sacrificial men. Jesus gave abundantly, and so can we. It might be hard to write that check or give that money away, but when you do, your heart is set free more and more from the cares of this world as you receive the joy of knowing that you have helped someone here on earth.

And truthfully, this will be one of the most rewarding experiences of your entire life. You will watch God provide for you as you financially prioritize His kingdom and demonstrate a generous heart. Just as He has always provided for Israel and the church, He will provide for you. This is one area God asked His people to test Him in, and He has proved Himself ever faithful. *"Bring the full tithe into the storehouse, that there may be food in my house. And thereby put me to the test, says the Lord of hosts, if I will not open the windows of heaven for you and pour down for you a blessing until there is no more need"* (Malachi 3:10).

Work

"Bondservants, obey in everything those who are your earthly masters, not by way of eye-service, as people-pleasers, but with sincerity of heart, fearing the Lord. Whatever you do, work heartily, as for the Lord and not for men, knowing that from the Lord you will receive the inheritance as your reward. You are serving the Lord Christ" (Colossians 3:22–24).

"Masters, treat your bondservants justly and fairly, knowing

that you also have a Master in heaven" (Colossians 4:1).

The godly Christian man should have a wonderful work ethic. As an employer of a massive workforce, Solomon observed, *"lazy people irritate their employers, like vinegar to the teeth or smoke in the eyes"* (Proverbs 10:26). If you've taken a swig of vinegar or been around a bonfire recently, you know what he's talking about. Instead, the Christian man understands that he is working for a greater, invisible master, God Himself. This energizes and motivates him to do an excellent job.

As Solomon stated, the lazy man irritates his employer. This can be done in a myriad of ways, but here are a few. The lazy man keeps his eye continually on that clock. He shows up late or just right on time. He rarely stays late, if ever. The lazy man refuses direction. The boss must prepare himself mentally every time he gives this man any word of correction. The lazy man allows his skills to decline. He refuses to learn, receive training, or gain any wisdom or ability that would make him more valuable to his organization. The lazy man brings a horrible attitude to work, bringing down the overall morale of the team. The lazy man is not team-oriented, instead being only concerned with what "his job" is, never thinking about what is best for the entire company or organization. The lazy man is not trustworthy. When he says yes, it actually means maybe. Sensitive information is catastrophic in his hands.

Instead, Christian men should be like Joseph who caused every one of his masters to prosper. This man might find himself promoted again and again due to his wonderful faithfulness and work ethic. *"Do you see a man skillful in his work? He will stand before kings; he will not stand before obscure men"* (Proverbs 22:29). He understands that he is earning a paycheck in this life, but also in that life which is to come with God. He realizes that faithfulness in the smallest matters is what God is looking for.

Additionally, the godly Christian man is a wonderful master. Like Boaz before him, his workers are well pleased at being under his supervision (Ruth 2:4). He does not exasperate his employees or team, instead he encourages them by bringing the best out of them. He commands respect and holds his workers accountable, but when faced with their poor performance, he does not discipline from a place of anger. This kind of man attracts the best of the best for his team, because everyone wants to work for him. He has a *"cool spirit"* (Proverbs 17:27) and is *"slow to anger"* (Proverbs 19:11).

Body

"For while bodily training is of some value, godliness is of value in every way, as it holds promise for the present life and also for the life to come" (1 Timothy 4:8).

We live in a body-conscious society. While the cultural standards for beauty might change from generation to generation, the pressure to conform to them is always constant. I pray for the women in our congregation as they are constantly bombarded with societal pressure to look and behave a certain way physically. But this pressure has not escaped men. The worship of athletes, an out of balance concern about our sexual experiences, and a general insecurity among men might be some of the factors that encourage us to pay such close attention to our health and physique.

As a former ridiculously average high school level athlete who still enjoys exercise today, I can understand some of the pressure to look and feel a certain way. In fact, I am very thankful for the friends in my life who have encouraged me toward healthy living. Still, it is important for us men to be balanced. As Paul stated in the text above, bodily training does have its place. My personal goal is to take my personal fitness seriously enough in order to do everything I can to be healthy enough provide for my family, enjoy my grandchildren, and effectively minister the Gospel for years to come. Additionally, athletics and physical training can be a great way to build camaraderie with other Christian brothers or to begin to connect with non-believing friends. Still, it is tempting for a man to place too much of a priority on his health or his physique. Even though many in our culture might worship the human body, we worship Jesus Christ, the one who will give us new bodies for all of eternity in His presence.

Perhaps this isn't even close to being an issue for you. Maybe you couldn't care less about your physique or your health. The book of Proverbs warns against a gluttonous life, so be careful (see Proverbs 23:20–21, 28:7). As I stated earlier, we are called to be stewards of all that God has entrusted to us, including our bodies. When it comes to our health, there are obviously factors way beyond our control, but a decent diet, regular exercise, and a refusal to poison our bodies with toxic drugs or alcohol abuse should be part of that stewardship.

Either way, if you experience pride or shame as a result of the way you look, your priorities are out of balance. Go back to your identity in Christ. The way you look is not what makes you or breaks you. Your strength and physique should not be your source of boldness or confidence. In the same way, weakness, sickness, or a few extra pounds ought not to devastate our morale. Receive the confidence that comes from being found in Christ by God, hearing Him say, *"This is my beloved son, in whom I am well pleased."*

Entertainment

"For many, of whom I have often told you and now tell you even with tears, walk as enemies of the cross of Christ. Their end is destruction, their god is their belly, and they glory in their shame, with minds set on earthly things" (Philippians 3:18–19).

We are men who live on planet Earth. Because of this, we will be presented with various time killers and forms of entertainment. Like money, the idea of entertainment is neither good nor evil, but neutral. I believe there was great joy and entertainment in the Garden of Eden, just as I believe there will be wonderful entertainment throughout eternity.

Still, it is important for the Christian man to have a discerning mind when it comes to his hobbies, interests, and various forms of entertainment. Some forms of entertainment are easy for believing men to receive. Various forms of music, sports, and intellectual pursuits are harmless enough. Other areas of entertainment need a little tweaking in order to be received by God's men. At times it is good for a Christian man to hit the fast-forward button, skip to the next track, or turn his head as the dance team does its thing during intermission. Additionally, there are obviously forms of entertainment a Christian man should never engage himself in. Strip clubs and casinos are not places the man of God should feel comfortable. Be discerning.

When it comes to entertainment, the word moderation comes to mind. Little girls don't dream of the day they are swept off their feet by a Prince Charming who will then proceed to play video games five hours a day. As stated earlier, there is a time, place, and even responsibility for physical training, but twenty-plus hours of training each week might be better off left with the single men and professional athletes. Again, you might love football, but football didn't die for you and shed its blood for you, so think carefully about what you're going to do on Sunday mornings.

Let me be clear, I definitely know how to relax and have a good time. Any of my friends could tell you that I know how to blow off some steam and get some good downtime. I take vacation time seriously, planning them in advance so that our family can look forward to them. Because much of my working life requires mental energy, I place a priority on physical exertion in my entertainment. Additionally, I quite often remember that I serve a God who instituted a weekly relaxation and worship day for the people of Israel. The key, however, is to live a balanced and moderate life in these areas. We should not talk about balance and moderation when it comes to serving the Lord, without ever applying that principle to our own finances or entertainment. Instead, we should flip that script by serving God wholeheartedly, using entertainment and down times as forms of rest to restore our souls.

Contentment

"Not that I am speaking of being in need, for I have learned in whatever situation I am to be content. I know how to be brought low, and I know how to abound. In any and every circumstance, I have learned the secret of facing plenty and hunger, abundance and need" (Philippians 4:11–12).

Paul learned how to be content in every condition of life. He had been well loved, but he had also experienced a deep poverty. He had been healthy, but he had also been sick. He had been exalted, but he had also been brought low. In the midst of these extreme highs and lows, Paul learned a wonderful secret— contentment. It is in this context that Paul uttered the famous words, "*I can do all things through him who strengthens me*" (Philippians 4:13).

When it comes to the lives we live on a daily basis, a great secret to our success will be contentment. Without contentment we will never find rest in our souls. We will instead bite, devour, scratch, and claw to get where we feel we need to be (Galatians 5:15). Remember, these lives are not our own. They were bought at a price and have been purchased by God. As the sovereign Lord of our lives, He determines what is right for each one of us. Pursue Him, engage with Him, and allow Him to lead your life and lifestyle. Learn how to be content in every stage and station of life.

Discontentment works hand in hand with temptation. The content man is able to resist the lies of temptation. At the core of sexual sin is some version of discontentment, sometimes with the spouse God has given you or an internal insecurity in your heart. The content man is able to flee sexual immorality. He is also able to spend, budget, save, and give well. Satisfied within his heart, this man operates with self-control and restraint financially. In every area of life, contentment aids and strengthens us. It keeps us from wrongful extremes and enables us to run full speed in the callings of God upon our lives.

Chapter 6: Your Relationships

"When the righteous increase, the people rejoice, but when the wicked rule, the people groan." (Proverbs 29:2).

In one sense, being a man is an incredible opportunity. This opportunity will be used to either build up or tear down. Our lives will be either constructive or destructive, but hardly neutral. As stated in Proverbs 29:2, the righteous man has a wonderful opportunity to bless the people around him. At the same time, even if a man begrudges it, because he is called to be a leader, any choice he makes to live a wicked life will cause great pain to the people around him and under his care.

Our Words

"With (our mouths) we bless our Lord and Father, and with it we curse people who are made in the likeness of God. From the same mouth come blessing and cursing. My brothers, these things ought not to be so." (James 3:9–10).

Because of the influential position many men occupy in the lives of others, it is important to take a hard look at the power of our words. James, whom I've just quoted, called the tongue *"a fire, a world of unrighteousness"* (James 3:6) and *"a restless evil, full of deadly poison"* (James 3:8). To him, the potential for great harm being done by our words is obvious. Yet many men feel otherwise. They find angry, vengeful, spiteful, or hateful words appropriate for communication. Make no mistake, our words can decimate lives, especially the lives of the people who are closest to us.

Instead, "*Let no corrupting talk come out of your mouths, but only such as is good for building up, as fits the occasion, that it may give grace to those who hear*" (Ephesians 4:29). Our speech should be filled with blessing. Those who listen to us should receive grace, edification, and be built up. Our words can "*exalt*" or "*overthrow*" a city (see Proverbs 11:11), while with lies and deceit, we can destroy our neighbor (see Proverbs 11:9). I am continually learning and trying to comprehend the power behind my words, especially with my wife, my children, and men who might look to me for guidance. In one sense it is scary, but in another sense it is an incredible opportunity.

Destructive Speech

One major form of destructive speech is **deceitfulness**. Indeed, "*lying lips are an abomination to the Lord*" (Proverbs 12:22). Satan is the father of lies (John 8:44) who produced the original lie (Genesis 3), so whenever we lie we are following in his slithery footsteps. When an employer lies about the poor performance of one of his employees, and instead chooses to gloss it over and make that person feel like he or she is doing a wonderful job, it can become a sore spot for the entire organization and a difficult situation to remedy down the line. When an employee lies about an ability, making it seem as if he or she is qualified for a task he or she knows little to nothing about, the productivity of the entire team will come to a screeching halt. When a man lies to his friend by refusing to confront him over poor habits that are destroying his marriage, he is actually aiding in the deterioration of a family. When a husband lies about the pressures he is experiencing in the workplace, instead telling his wife that everything is just fine, things will eventually boil over and get ugly, perhaps in the form of an extramarital affair or flashes of anger. Obviously, it is important to be truthful with those we love.

Another form of destructive speech is **slander**, which is obviously a form of deceitfulness. *"Whoever goes about slandering reveals secrets; therefore do not associate with a simple babbler"* (Proverbs 20:19). Gossip is indeed a killer, and in this digital age, it can wreck a person in no time at all. The slanderous man is looking to take down those above him and around him by telling tales. He is constantly looking for dirt and trying to expose sin. His wife, children, and friends are often targets of his whisperings. No word is safe with him, so the people in his life refuse to confide in him.

Anger-filled words are another form of incredibly disruptive speech. Biblically, we are told to *"make no friendship with a man given to anger, nor go with a wrathful man"* (Proverbs 22:24). Once an unrighteous anger takes over your heart and conversation, whatever you were trying to communicate gets hijacked and a different message altogether is delivered. Your actual words might even be incredibly instructive and helpful, but in your anger and wrath all you can do is destroy. No matter how reasonable your argument might be, if we can see the vein popping out of your forehead while you say it, we likely won't receive it well. I have often heard the Holy Spirit ask me the same question God asked of Jonah, *"is it right for you to be angry?"* (Jonah 4:4, 9). And, even though there is such a thing as anger without sin and righteous anger, more often than not, the correct answer is no. Losing your cool in any conversation is like derailing a speeding train. It will create disaster that is difficult to repair.

Constructive Speech

As God's men we have an opportunity to speak righteous

and good words in a timely and controlled way in order to build up our hearers. We must *"let (our) speech always be gracious, seasoned with salt"* (Colossians 4:6). Words that are filled with grace and full of the Gospel will edify the people around us, which will bring incredible glory to God. Remember, *"the mouth of the righteous is a fountain of life"* (Proverbs 10:11), so you and I have a great opportunity to give life with our words. Let me give you three examples.

One way to use our words constructively is by speaking **pleasant** and **good** words to others. Words like this can bring *"health to the bones"* and lift the anxiety and depression of others, instead causing gladness (Proverbs 16:24, 12:25). We are presented opportunities quite constantly where a person's heart is on the verge of heading in one of two directions: either being encouraged and helped or heading into depression and despair. In these moments it is important for us to speak pleasant and good words into the heart of this person, rescuing that soul from the abyss of despair.

Another way to use our words constructively is by delivering a **timely** word. A timely word is the right word at the right time. *"A word in season, how good it is!"* (Proverbs 15:23). Although I'm not entirely sure what apples of gold in settings of silver look like, I'm fairly certain they're worth a pretty penny, and Scripture tells us they compare to aptly spoken words (Proverbs 25:11–12). Knowing when to speak and what to say is an absolute gift and skill. When your children are discouraged, your wife is distraught, or your coworkers are stressed, you have an opportunity. At that moment, use your words for good.

Finally, **measured** words are another wonderful way to use our speech for constructive purposes. To give a soft answer with a calm spirit is to use knowledge rightly (Proverbs 15:1-2, 17:27). Make no mistake, there will be moments our words sting a little. Every constructive word that comes out of our mouth won't be initially positive. Especially as we talk to those whom we are in positions of authority over, it is right for us to, in a tempered and measured way, speak the truth to them in love (Ephesians 4:15).

In any case, it is important for us to consider our words in every important relationship we will carry here on earth. We will give an account for every word we speak, so we ought to speak them as if God is listening. We have such an incredible opportunity with so many people, and, as our words can build up or tear down, it is important for us to use our words to encourage and help the kingdom of God advance.

Marriage

"Let marriage be held in honor among all" (Hebrews 13:4).

Since a large portion of the population in America will marry at some point, and since marriage is the beginning of a family, the linchpin to a healthy society, this is a massive subject. Broken hearts, dysfunctional homes, and rising divorce rates often cause us to forget that marriage was a perfect gift from God in the Garden of Eden. Marriage is a sacred gift from God that reflects the relationship between Christ and His church. God does not take marriage lightly, and neither should you.

Jesus Talks Marriage

Before sin entered the world, God instituted the first marriage. In fact, Jesus goes to great lengths to remind the Pharisees and others of that first marriage (Mark 10:1–11).

These Pharisees, like many in Israel, had centered their ideas of marriage on the law, but Jesus longed to take them back to the original marriage in Genesis 1-2. From that original marriage, I believe we can learn some foundational lessons about how to have successful marriages in our day and age.

Be softhearted. *"And Jesus said to them, 'Because of your hardness of heart he wrote you this commandment. But from the beginning of creation, God made them male and female"* (Mark 10:5–6). Jesus clearly taught that hardheartedness was to blame for the *"certificate of divorce"* passage in Deuteronomy 24. Had the Pharisees been "softhearted" they would have been more concerned with God's ideal than pushing the limits on divorce. A softhearted marriage will long for God's best. A softhearted person longs to know God's ideal scenario. A softhearted person is willing to work things out with their spouse, opening their hearts to them.

I've found the importance of softheartedness in marriage cannot be understated. Marriage is not a magical experience that just works, but instead a relationship that takes time, effort, and commitment. One of the ingredients a healthy marriage will have is true softheartedness toward one another. If you are a married man, you need to be the initiator of this softheartedness. Don't insecurely wait for your wife to initiate this, but instead humble out and open your heart to her.

Know your roles. *"But from the beginning of creation, 'God made them male and female"* (Mark 10:6). In successful marriages the husband and wife recognize they are different from one another and that those differences lead them to very distinct roles. For everything else each spouse brings to the relationship, the husband understands he is called to provide, protect, lead, and love his wife. The wife understands that she is to follow, support, respect, and love her husband (see Ephesians 5:22-33).

As a godly Christian man, take your role and responsibility seriously. You aren't a bully or a boss in your home. You are a loving servant leader who is required to prefer your wife and your children above yourself. Your leadership should be gentle, kind, and other-centered. In the same way Jesus loves his church, you love your bride sacrificially by laying down your life for her (Ephesians 5:25). Like Jesus before you, you are not concerned with your own rights and privileges, but concerned with laying down your life for your bride. Your love actually sanctifies and cleanses your bride (Ephesians 5:26). In other words, she is better off by knowing you and actually grows as a person through her relationship with you.

Create a new circle. "*Therefore a man shall leave his father and mother and hold fast to his wife*" (Mark 10:7). Many call this the "leave and cleave" principle. This obviously takes maturity on the part of the man, but also an ability to defend the new circle that God has formed with his wife. Unwanted advice, ungodly counsel, and wicked friendships should not be allowed inside that inner circle. It must be protected.

Because of their enormously long lifespans, Adam and Eve were likely married for over nine hundred years. Since God created them directly, one advantage they had over modern marriages is they never had to deal with meddling parents. A boy will complain to his mother about his marriage, but a man will protect his inner circle. A boy will complain about his wife to his father, but a man will guard her reputation. Certainly, there are seasons in a marriage where it is good to invite others in for godly counsel and encouragement. Often, the best way for this to occur is through mutual agreement with your spouse about who to talk to and invite in for help, but guard your inner circle.

Cultivate oneness. *"And the two shall become one flesh. So they are no longer two but one flesh"* (Mark 10:8). In marriage much of your personal identity is lost and you become one with your spouse. Marriages tend to break down when people behave as two single individuals with distinct and separate goals. Too many women and men are running off attempting to "find themselves," when all they really need to discover is found inside their relationship with their spouse. When oneness is cultivated physically, emotionally, spiritually, and practically, the marriage has a good chance for great success. When pride rules the day, a spouse hates the idea of being one with their mate, instead choosing to focus on their individuality.

This oneness with your spouse must be cultivated. In addition to being passionate lovers, I believe husbands and wives ought to be best friends. The wife in the Song of Solomon—an intensely romantic book—refers to her husband as her friend (Song of Solomon 5:16). Learn how to be a good friend to your wife. Date her regularly. Listen to her. Take notes about her. Like you, she is an ever-developing creature, so learn about her. Talk about what God is showing you and hear what God is showing her. Be friends. Cultivate your oneness. This oneness is often ruined when we broadcast the failures of our wives or become easily offended because of our insecurities (Proverbs 16:28, 17:9, 27:6). Instead, strive to provide a safe environment for your wife to live in with you.

Be covenantal. *"What therefore God has joined together, let not man separate"* (Mark 10:9). Ultimately, even though the church and state are involved in marriage, God is the one who presides over every married couple. In other words, God is the tie that binds us together. Not the state, not the church, but God. This view allows a person to see their marriage as an act of devotion, worship, obedience, and stewardship toward God. A covenantal attitude, rather than a contractual attitude, will lead a person to never give up or never give in on their marriage.

In a day where seemingly everyone has an opinion on how to have a successful marriage, only Jesus Christ is able to truly take us to the very core of the matter. As our designer, He understands exactly what is necessary within marriage. Let's obey Him in our quest for excellent marriages.

The Good Husband

The good husband holds his wife out as his standard of beauty and enjoys her and her alone sexually (Proverbs 5:15–20). He is a covenantal man who is not going to go back on his promise. When he said, "till death do us part," he actually meant it. Like Job before him, this man makes a covenant with his own eyes, so he will not lust after other women or gaze at them on his computer screen (Job 31:1). He understands adultery begins in the heart, so he protects and guards his heart, making sure he pours his affection and attention out upon his wife. His wife feels incredibly free around him, emotionally, spiritually, physically, and sexually.

She grows under his care and love. She feels protected by him. She feels like he loves her and would do anything for her. When he makes a financial decision, she doesn't blink, because she knows he will put her and the family first. She is thankful for the friends he has selected, because they are godly and encourage him in his walk with God and relationship with her. She is confident that if he were to slip into sin he would receive the rebukes of spiritual leadership in his life. She is happy because he isn't an island, but an open book, allowing Christ-like men access into his life. She trusts this man.

The Bad Husband

The bad husband is cruel in all his ways. The pinnacle of his cruelty is that he strays from his home, like a bird that strays from its nest (Proverbs 27:8). He is intentionally always away from the house, working ridiculously long hours, at play with all of his hobbies, and out with his friends. Even when he is home, he really isn't. He occupies himself with his iPhone or video games or the television. He basically lives like a single man. He cares not for oneness with his wife and doesn't think twice about building an inner circle with her. His heart is not open to her. He is a closed door. He accumulates bad friends and has a bad temper. Alcohol and drugs are often his coping mechanism. He doesn't lead well, doesn't like church, and isn't willing to submit to any spiritual authority. His eyes are constantly wandering, and pornography is a part of his regular routine. This man is destroying a life.

His wife wilts under his leadership. She prays daily for God to change her husband's heart, but like Pharaoh before him, his heart will not budge and only gets worse. She knows she can't talk to him about money, the kids, or her thoughts. It's hard enough feeling secure as a woman in this day and age, but her marriage to him only makes her feel more insecure with her appearance. She often sits alone at church and feels she has to attend an all-female small group because there's no chance he would ever attend one with her. She grows discouraged watching him spend their money on his pursuits and toys. She is so tired.

Serve Her

Jesus said, "*If anyone would be first, he must be last of all and servant of all*" (Mark 9:35). When a man takes a wife, he is taking a role of leadership. He is becoming first. So Jesus tells us that we must become last and servant of all in that leadership position and role. I want to encourage you to love and serve your wife. Open up your heart to her. Bless her. Pray with her. Even if you are married to a difficult woman, take the time to invest in your relationship in whatever way possible.

One of the best gifts you could ever give to your wife is a strong relationship with God. If you are the leader and she is under your care, she desperately needs you to be under the leadership of God. If you're not, it's a scary place for her to live, and she will be tempted to act out in response to your lack of submission to God by taking matters into her own hands. Being a Bible-loving, church-going, in fellowship, praying man is a gift to your wife and a wonderful service to her. You will never be perfect, but at least you'll be growing.

Helps

Prayer. Christina and I have discovered that one of the most intimate things we can do together is pray. Before God we are bearing our souls and exposing our hearts to one another in a very revealing way. To pray for our marriage, our children, our finances, our church, our extended family, our friendships, and the goals that are attached to each one of them is a wonderful experience. It not only unites and educates us, but in prayer, we also receive help from God.

Dates. From the very beginning of our marriage, Christina and I have had a weekly date night. A date night might sound cliché, but for us these nights have been wonderful. Obviously, the addition of children means we have to plan a little more in advance, but we still enjoy a weekly night together. As a general rule, we don't go to the movies as we want to use that time to talk to one another. Additionally, this doesn't have to be an expensive endeavor. In fact, if it's regular, it usually can't be. But with careful planning and thought, these can be wonderful times and very helpful to the marriage.

Planning. By nature I am a planner. Although we haven't done this every single year of our marriage, Christina and I have been helped by having a yearly planning meeting where we set our schedule and talk about goals for our marriage, finances, children, friendships, and church life. This is typically an all-day affair where we get it all out on the table. This is also the time we normally come up with our yearly budget, subject to change month-to-month.

Budget. This one bears a little repeating. Christina saw firsthand how financial disagreements can harm a marriage during her childhood, so it has been very important to her that we be on the same page financially. I couldn't agree more and have been very glad for her zeal in this area. I cannot stress how important a financial plan has been to our marriage. It relieves stress, pressures, and disagreements. Our pattern is to create a budget each year and review it each month.

Trips. Trips have been a wonderful way to keep the spark alive in our marriage. God has put some wonderful people in our lives who are willing to take our children for a night or two (or more), and we have taken full advantage of those relationships. Since Christina is a busy mother who by necessity operates at a frenetic pace, it is especially important to get her out of town and away from her responsibilities from time to time.

It is important, especially during the child-raising years, to continually have fun with each other and cultivate your personal relationship to one another. A day is coming, sooner than you expected, where your house will be empty again, and you will be left with only each other. Whatever stage you are in, take the bull by the horns, be the man in the relationship, and make sure to have a lot of fun with your wife.

Fatherhood

"Pray then like this: 'Our Father in heaven, hallowed be your name'" (Matthew 6:9).

It is altogether wonderful and shocking to know that God shares his title of "father" with man, especially since good fathers are a declining commodity. With many babies born to unmarried mothers and many children living without their biological father, Christian men have a wonderful opportunity to set the pace and demonstrate what an excellent father looks like. As I begin this section, I have in my mind the faces of three or four wonderful fathers who attend the church I pastor. Their gentle leadership of their children throughout the years has produced wonderful fruit. *"The glory of children is their fathers"* (Proverbs 17:6), a statement which certainly holds true in the families I am thinking of.

Perhaps you are a young man, and family is yet in the future for you. Even though the beginning of a family could be a mere hop, skip, and a jump away, it feels like the last thing on your mind. I encourage you to buckle down and take preparation for fatherhood seriously. It is one of the most important ministries and callings you will ever engage in.

Perhaps you are in the heat of the battle, currently fathering little children or teenagers within your home. You might feel as if it is too late to prepare, wishing you had taken the time to receive better instruction on parenting before you headed into it. Like nearly all of us, you are learning on the fly, so don't sweat it, and allow the Spirit of God to speak to you. Perhaps a nugget of truth or a pearl of wisdom might stand out and strengthen you in your current fatherly role.

Perhaps your children are out of the home and fully grown. I'm sure you look back on the years your children were in your home with fondness, but with moments of regret. No earthly man has ever fathered perfectly like our Father in heaven, so let me encourage you to receive the grace of God and run toward the very important fatherhood role you still occupy.

Delight in Children

"My son, do not despise the Lord's discipline or be weary of his reproof, for the Lord reproves him whom he loves, as a father the son in whom he delights" (Proverbs 3:11–12).

One of the first things I would like to communicate about our role as fathers is the need to delight in our children. Proverbs 3:11–12 makes it clear that our heavenly Father loves his children and delights in them. Before a father begins to discipline his children, he must love them, like them, and delight in them. Paul exhorts fathers by telling us, "*do not provoke your children to anger*" (Ephesians 6:4). One of the surest ways to provoke our children to anger and wrath is to discipline and instruct them without delighting in them. This is a surefire way to exasperate and discourage our children, something Paul warns against (Colossians 3:21).

It is important to remember that God delights in us before He disciplines us. He sent His only begotten son to us, proving His love for us. It is in response to the love of God as revealed on the cross that we open up to His leadership in our lives. Notice that the delight and love of God was sacrificial in nature. The cross is not left up to personal interpretation, but is instead a clear and obvious sign which demonstrates God's love for His people. As fathers, our delight must be visible and obvious to our children, just as the cross of Christ clarifies God's love for us.

Time for Children

"For everything there is a season, and a time for every matter under heaven: a time to be born...die...plant...pluck up what is planted...kill...heal...break down...build up...weep...laugh...mourn...dance...cast away stones...gather stones together;...embrace...refrain from embracing...seek...lose...keep...cast away...tear...sew...keep silence...speak...love...hate...war...peace" (Ecclesiastes 3:1–8).

I know of no better way to delight in my children than by giving them my time. Obviously, this looks different for each child and each season of that child's life. While all of my daughters have enjoyed wrestling at different stages of their lives, I don't expect this form of physical contact to be their preferred method forever (I do, however, expect to snuggle with them during football games until the day I die!). Going on daddy dates together, taking trips together, reading books before bedtime, having conversations together over ice cream, and playing sports together are just a few of the things we do in our household. What my children really long for is me, not stuff.

In whatever season of life you and your children are in, I would encourage you to make time for them. For many of you, this will mean getting them onto your calendar, like the year I scheduled myself to pick up our oldest daughter from school every Friday in order to recap her week and take her for ice cream. This little gesture cost me $1.07 each week and, more importantly to her, my time. She still thanks me for those short times we spent together.

This might also mean building family times into your life. For us, this includes family days and a night each week we have a little family church service together. These weekly times become habit and routine, ensuring Christina and me space in life to be with our children. Throughout the day there will be numerous times you can be available to your children. Putting them to bed, sitting with them, reading to them, asking them questions; whatever it takes, give your children your time.

Additionally, as much as we must fight to give our children a good quantity of our time, we must also be sure to give them quality time. In other words, we need to have moments we are free from distraction to enjoy our children. During one busy season of life, we instituted what we called Amish Fridays in order to ensure one day per week we could be together without the distraction of phone calls, text messages, emails, or the Internet. These days were a precious time to refocus our energies on our children and recharge our batteries at the same time. Maybe technology isn't much of a hindrance for you, but make sure the time you spend with your children is time you are actually present. To be there bodily, yet distracted mentally, is not ideal.

I should briefly note that many parents have taken this to an illogical extreme by basically worshipping their children. They prioritize their children at the expense of their marriage, church, work, health, and responsibilities. This parent would never dream of missing a game or recital. Understand that the good father will usually be present at such occasions, but your children need to know you also have a priority for your spouse and a responsibility to your work, for instance. Part of training them well is teaching them by example that you have other responsibilities to care for.

Pray for Children

I love David's prayer for his son Solomon: *"Grant to Solomon my son a whole heart that he may keep your commandments, your testimonies, and your statutes, performing all, and that he may build the palace for which I have made provision"* (1 Chronicles 29:19). The godly Christian man will pray for his children. Just like Jesus prayed from the mountaintop over His disciples as they strained at the oars on the Sea of Galilee, so a good father will lift up his children to God (Mark 6:48).

Like David, it is a good idea to pray for your children's **spiritual health**. Paul, a spiritual father of the Ephesian church, prayed for them to *"have strength to comprehend with all the saints what is the breadth and length and height and depth, and to know the love of Christ that surpasses knowledge, that you may be filled with all the fullness of God"* (Ephesians 3:18–19). Praying for the spiritual protection of our children is always a good idea. Lifting up their hearts to God, asking Him to open their hearts and minds to His glory and grace, is a wonderful way for a father to intercede.

Like many fathers throughout the Gospels, it is also a good idea to pray for the **physical health** of your children (see Mark 5:23, John 4:46–53). It gives me a wonderful piece of mind to ask God to give my family health in the future, especially when we are healthy in the present. Health should not be taken for granted, so preemptively praying for future health is a wonderful way to trust God. Should that day come where one of us falls seriously ill, however, I will kick my prayers into high gear and call for the elders of the church to pray for my children that they might be healed (James 5), at the end of the day trusting God and His sovereign plan.

Job was an example of a wonderful father who prayed for his children to stand strong in the face of **temptation**. After their days of feasting had ended *"he would rise early in the morning and offer burnt offerings according to the number of them all. For Job said, 'It may be that my children have sinned, and cursed God in their hearts.'" Thus Job did continually"* (Job 1:5). One of the difficulties of being a father is letting your children go. You know that the world is a difficult place to live in, full of temptation. The godly father prays for his children to be able to stand strong in the face of temptation and adversity.

One other important area to pray for our children is in the realm of their **relationships**. Outside of their relationship with you, your children's friendships have the opportunity to shape them most deeply. Pray often for your kids to have godly friends who will encourage them to know and honor Jesus. Pray for them, that when they are surrounded with friends who do not love the Lord, they will be able to stand strong. Additionally, pray for their future spouse, if it be God's will for them to marry. Cry out to God for their sanctification and knowledge of God's will for their lives. You aren't the parent of these friends and future spouses, but you can certainly do battle for them in prayer.

As a side note, allow your children to hear you pray for them from time to time. This isn't an opportunity for you to manipulate them in any way, shape, or form, but for them to hear your genuine heart for them as you lift them up in prayer.

Teach Children

"My son, do not forget my teaching, but let your heart keep my commandments, for length of days and years of life and peace they will add to you" (Proverbs 3:1–2).

Christian fathers are to bring up their children *"in the discipline and instruction of the Lord"* (Ephesians 6:4). Just as our heavenly Father teaches us, so earthly fathers are to instruct their children. Vast portions of the book of Proverbs are merely the teachings of a father to his son. If we do not input into our children's lives, someone else will. Unfortunately, there is a long line of people who do not share our biblical values and who are willing to take up the slack.

As a Bible teacher and a Christian man, I consider it an honor, responsibility, and challenge to teach my children the word of God. The challenge part comes in the fact that I want the word of God to always be fresh and interesting to them, for that is what it truly is. For that reason, I buy them all of the children's Bibles they like, and try to teach them age-appropriate lessons from God's word. Especially in the early years, a father has a wonderful opportunity to lay a foundation of biblical understanding in his children's lives.

When it comes to children, one of the best forms of teaching is on-the-fly teaching throughout the day. When teaching the law to their children, parents in Israel were to "*teach them diligently to your children, and shall talk of them when you sit in your house, and when you walk by the way, and when you lie down, and when you rise*" (Deuteronomy 6:7). In other words, the word of God was to be in constant discussion and dialogue throughout the day.

Fathers, this does not mean we are called to teach our children all of the "right" verses. They need to know more than Colossians 3:20 ("*Children, obey your parents in everything, for this pleases the Lord*") and Deuteronomy 5:16 ("*Honor your father and your mother*"). When teaching our children the word of God, it is important to embrace the idea that the Gospel and Christianity are not tools to get good behavior out of children.

Ultimately, we aren't looking for mere external reformation, but instead we are longing for regeneration in their lives, a regeneration which leads to true transformation of their character. In other words, beware of the danger of moralizing every single text in order for them to get a little "lesson" out of it. Just teach them what the Bible says. Take them through the stories of the Old Testament. Show them the Gospels. Give them the history found in the book of Acts. Share your eschatological framework with them. They will be fascinated by it and can handle a lot more than we might think.

Dad, the buck stops with you when it comes to your children's instruction in the word of God. Don't leave it to Sunday school or children's church or youth group. You are their pastor. Teach them. Sit down with them. Perhaps you should consider having a weekly time designated where you take your family through a book of the Bible and explain what it means to your own heart, giving them opportunities to read scriptures, share artwork or poems that pertain to your text, and give prayer requests. I assure you, this is one of the manliest things you will ever do.

Protect Children

"In the fear of the Lord one has strong confidence, and his children will have a refuge" (Proverbs 14:26).

As a Father, God is a place of refuge for His children (Proverbs 14:26). The godly Christian man will be a wonderful refuge for his children. When you think about it, the world is not a very safe place for kids. Neglect, abuse, poverty, molestation, fornication, and rape are modern concerns for children. Not only that, but the information age we are living in, one where every form of evil can seemingly find its way into the family living room, requires a father to be diligent to provide a place of protection for his children.

Kids are safe with a dad who fears God. One of my favorite New Testament characters is a man named Philip. Philip was filled with the Holy Spirit and could be called one of the first deacons in the early church. He wound up preaching the Gospel to an important man from Ethiopia. This eventually brought him to Caesarea Philippi, where he lived the rest of his life with his *"four virgin daughters who prophesied"* (Acts 21:9 NKJV). I believe Philip had something to do with their sexual purity. I believe he was involved in their lives by protecting his daughters.

As stated earlier, fathers cannot be with their children at all times. Obviously, our children have to live their own lives and will ultimately be held responsible for their own actions. Still, a good father will involve himself in their lives, especially during their teen and preteen years. A good father won't allow his children to be left unsupervised in the homes of others he doesn't know. If there is an age he allows his children to date, the father will be intimately involved, setting the boundaries and inserting himself into the relationships. A good father will prayerfully think through things like sleepovers, Internet, and smart phones for his children.

Jesus said, *"whoever causes one of these little ones who believe in Me to stumble, it would be better for him if a millstone were hung around his neck, and he were thrown into the sea"* (Mark 9:42). The godly father who discovers his son struggling with pornography will not subsequently give his son a full-fledged Internet connection complete with personal computer in the privacy of his own bedroom. Do your kids a solid. Get them the filters, accountability, and boundaries they need. They may bristle at first, but these actions tell them that you love them.

Train Children

"For what son is there whom a father does not chasten?" (Hebrews 12:7).

One of the most constant responsibilities of a father is to give discipline to his children. Now, I've already talked about disciplining your children, teaching them the dictates and standards of God, but discipline is a different form of teaching. The best discipline comes from a man who submits to God's discipline over his life. If a man is willing to hear the gentle rebuke of God's Spirit, he will gain the authority to speak into his children's lives.

The most important factor in giving discipline to children is consistency. If you fluctuate wildly in your response to their acts of disobedience, you will have successfully created a confusing environment for your children to grow up in. However, if you discipline them for the same things in the same way with a gentle spirit, you will have given them a safe environment in which to learn and grow. Only to put forth one example, my children have been disciplined for the same four rules their entire lives: they are not to be disrespectful to their parents, be unkind to others, have an unpleasant attitude, or be disobedient to their parents.

Christina and I have experienced how hard it is to be consistent in our discipline, mostly due to the frenetic pace of life and our own unwillingness to stop and take the time for necessary correction, but we have been largely rewarded for a general consistency of our discipline with our children.

There is a huge difference between punishment and discipline. Our heavenly Father does not punish us. Instead, He chose to punish His own Son with the punishment we rightfully deserved. Now, we are in a place where we receive the loving and gentle discipline of God, which is absent of any and all wrath. Remember this as you discipline your children. Whatever plan you put together for instructing and disciplining them, remember that it is for their training, not for their punishment.

A Demoniac's Dad

Partly through observation and partly through carrying out my own fatherly duties, God has placed a burden in my heart for fathers. I truly and honestly believe that many of the social ills facing our world and nation would disappear or lessen if there were a widespread return to the true and biblical meaning of fatherhood.

In Mark 9:14-29 we observe a wonderful father, who, through personal revival in his own soul, coupled with necessity in the life of his child, was driven to the feet of Jesus. His problem was immense. His son was demon possessed. He didn't know what else to do, so he brought his son to Jesus. After a brief conversation, Jesus delivered his son from that demonic influence. It is a very moving passage when seen through the lens of a loving father. Here are a few elements about this father we should observe:

He repented of his sin. Whatever had led his family and his son into demonic oppression and possession was cast off by this father as he watched his son reach this moment of desperation. Good fathers will repent of sin.

He prayed for his son. This father knew he needed to intercede for his child. Good fathers will pray for their kids.

He protected his son. This man saw demons ripping his son apart, but would not sit idly by. He knew he needed to be active in bringing his son to Jesus. Good fathers protect their kids by bringing them to Jesus any way they can.

He believed God for his son. Although the man also confessed unbelief regarding his son, he did have a measure of belief in what Jesus could do for his child. It is important for parents to believe that Jesus is able to work in the lives of their children. Good fathers believe in God's work for their kids.

Being a dad, I understand that perfection is impossible. I am, after all, a fallible human being who is prone to error and mistakes. I am thankful my children have a loving heavenly Father who is perfect and holy in all of His ways. That said, I invite God's men to join me in the pursuit of being excellent and biblical fathers. Let us pray for God to accomplish this work in our lives!

Friends

"A friend loves at all times, and a brother is born for adversity" (Proverbs 17:17).

I read an article recently about a professional football player who, a few years back, took his own life. In interviewing some of his old teammates for the article, the author found that they really didn't know what was happening with their teammate. Week after week these men would "go to war" together, but they knew little of each other's lives. They spoke of a brotherhood, but something was lacking.

We need friends. We have been made in the image of a God who is triune (Genesis 1:27). He has perfect fellowship within His triune Godhead. This same God looked at man in his original state and determined that the only thing wrong with him was that he was alone (Genesis 2:18). Any solid Christian man should desire to be a good friend and select good friends. Isolation is unhealthy and unwise, so we are sickly and foolish if we avoid the godly friendships God has for us (Proverbs 18:1). Throughout the different seasons of life, we will need other godly men to lean upon and strengthen us for the life God has called us to.

I cannot imagine passing through singleness, my school years, my early ministry years, marriage, child-raising, or pastoral work without a support system of good and godly friends. By friends I mean men who are in a similar season and stage of life as you, men you have mutually chosen to enter into friendship with (not just some guy who won't leave you alone). Your relationship is reciprocal. Like David and Jonathan, both of you have something to offer the other.

One of the chief reasons God wants you to have solid friends in your lives is to help you with your motivation and walk with God. *"The righteous should choose his friends carefully, For the way of the wicked leads them astray"* (Proverbs 12:26 NKJV). This means the wise man will search out, investigate, and carefully select his friends. Even though loud and rebellious dudes might seem like a lot of fun to be around, they are an absolute cancer. The wise man understands that his friends will have power to lead him toward good or toward evil. The wise man also understands that hanging out with fools will only rub off on him, making him more foolish (Proverbs 13:20). One way to become wise is to associate with wise people, so be careful what kind of friends you select.

For his part, God understands your friends will shape you in one way or another, just as *"iron sharpens iron, and one man sharpens another"* (Proverbs 27:17). Look for friends who will sharpen you through stimulating discussions, valid criticisms, challenging suggestions, and fresh viewpoints. In other words, you need to find men who will make you better as a result of spending time with them. Like Timothy and Silas for Paul in Corinth, we should be stirred up by the Spirit of God as a result of spending time with our friends (Acts 18:5).

Fortunately, the Bible gives us ample material to consider when selecting our friends. God doesn't leave us to our own feelings to decide whether a man would be "good" for us or not. If a man is a slanderer or dishonest, we should walk away (Proverbs 12:28). If he is a man given to wrath and anger, he has some issues to work out before you let him into your life in a close way (Proverbs 22:24). If he is a glutton who constantly feeds his own flesh and desires, he isn't worth spending time with (Proverbs 28:7). And if he is a sexually loose individual, I would encourage you to run away as fast as you can (Proverbs 29:3).

On the other hand, God tells us what kind of man we should be looking to hang out with. Loyalty and trustworthiness are the prime characteristics for us to look for in potential friends (Proverbs 18:24). A simple reading of the book of Acts should encourage you to find the right kind of friends, men who will stir you up to serve the living God.

If we really lay our lives down for the Lord, we are sure to experience intense trials and seasons of difficulty. It is then we are going to need solid friends who will encourage us in the path we have selected, rather than friends who will tell us to take it easy and turn from the call of God upon our lives. Pray with your friends. Open your heart to your friends. Tell them of your struggles and your dreams. Hold one another up in prayer. Support each other's families. This life is a war— support one another in it.

Responsibility

Again, being a man is a huge responsibility but a huge opportunity. We have the chance to influence lives for all of eternity. The weight and power of our words and actions is incredible.

When I first started walking with God, my father shared with me a story from 1 Chronicles about a man named Jabez. Apparently Jabez had caused quite a bit of pain for his mother at his birth, and his name indicated as much. When grown, however, Jabez prayed to God, *"Oh that you would bless me and enlarge my border, and that your hand might be with me, and that you would keep me from harm so that it might not bring me pain!"* (1 Chronicles 4:10). Jabez wanted to be a blessing to everyone around him. This is the righteous plea of the godly man.

Since then I have prayed this prayer, not for the purpose

of large borders, but for the purpose of blessing the people around me. I am fully aware my life could be a curse to many or a blessing to many. I long for my relationships to thrive as a result of their proximity to my life. I want my words to build up. I long to be a fruitful tree that benefits many.

Chapter 7: Your World

"Moreover, he must be well thought of by outsiders, so that he may not fall into disgrace, into a snare of the devil" (1 Timothy 3:7).

Outside of his relationships with God, self, family, friends, and church, the man of God will interact with various types of people during his brief stay here on earth. It is important for a godly man to behave with integrity in his treatment of others. We are to give honor to those to whom it is due, so it makes sense for us to be respectful, kind, and loving to all people (Romans 13:7). Because humans are made in the image of God and still carry a remnant of that image with them, it is only right for us to honor all of mankind in one way or another (Genesis 1:27). Practically speaking, the Bible gives us some direct instructions on how we are to treat different groups of people.

Mankind

"So God created man in his own image, in the image of God he created him; male and female he created them" (Genesis 1:27).

God desires for us to have a compassionate love and healthy respect for other people. As stated, they are image bearers of God and are, in one sense, our brothers and sisters. The precursor to the feeding of the five thousand on the shores of the Sea of Galilee is the compassion of Jesus for the crowds as he saw them like sheep without a shepherd (Mark 6:34). I doubt Peter would have preached the lifesaving Gospel on the day of Pentecost if he hadn't caught a little bit of that Christ-like compassion and allowed it to burn within his heart for the massive crowd that had gathered together (Acts 2). While it might be easy for Christians to live a defensive, angry, and frustrated existence in this world, God calls us to be dignified and loving in our response to it.

Believe in People's Potential

Years ago I was part of a small group who would regularly go to our city center in order to pray for people. We weren't praying highly public pharisaical-style prayers, but would merely break up into groups of two or three, find a café table or street bench, and pray for the people around us. We were careful not to draw attention to ourselves, but to look as natural and conversational as possible.

Although I have not repeated this practice often in my life, it did serve as a wonderful illustration of believing in the potential of others. In other words, as I prayed for different people around me, I found myself praying for their conversion and so much more. I truly believed that many of the people around me had futures as pastors, missionaries, church leaders, evangelists, and healthy fathers and mothers. This simple exercise helped me see that my heart could easily become jaded to the people around me, believing the absolute worst about them. Since *"love believes all things"* it is good for us to see the possibility of what God might do in a person's life, no matter how difficult this person might be for us personally (1 Corinthians 13:7).

In a world looking for superheroes, icons, and idols, people all around us can be true life changers for good. Paul did whatever he could to win men: *"For though I am free from all, I have made myself a servant to all, that I might win more of them"* (1 Corinthians 9:19). He made himself as a

Jew, as one outside of the law, and as one who is weak in order save some (1 Corinthians 9:20–22). Important to this mission is a vision for the potential the men and women around us carry. They were made in the image of God, so if regeneration occurs in their hearts, the sky is the limit when it comes to their potential.

Aspire to Peace

We are to *"aspire to live quietly, and to mind your own affairs"* (1 Thessalonians 4:11). Paul spoke this in the context of church life, but it is a good maxim for our attitude on living in this world as well. *"If possible, so far as it depends on you, live peaceably with all"* (Romans 12:18). Far from being a bunch of punks who provoked a fight, the first- century church merely preached the Gospel and, often the fight came to them. This is often typified in the life of men like Paul and Peter who caught the attention of government officials, religious authorities, and idolaters.

However, we should not overlook men like Philip who lived godly lives for long stretches of time in one place (Acts 21:9). We are to pray *"for kings and all who are in high positions, that we may lead a peaceful and quiet life, godly and dignified in every way"* (1 Timothy 2:2). A Christian man should be a wonderful addition to any community. Since he is at peace with God, he is able to add to the peace of the community.

Interest in People

Obviously, people are radically different from one another. Not only do personalities vary from man to man, but wildly different styles, upbringings, and backgrounds produce a seemingly endless stream of unique men and women. When insecurity and fear get in the way, we often see different kinds of people as threats. Instead, we should realize the infinite and multifaceted nature of God. The God of order is also intensely creative. He created nutrients to sustain man, but also taste buds so man could enjoy that sustenance. He organized the seasons, but also made them wonderfully beautiful. With His infinite imagination, He placed all kinds of wonderful animals upon the earth and in the ocean, but also gave man less glamorous animals like livestock in order to help sustain human life.

That said, humans ought to be interesting to us. Our primary concern as Christian men is for the Gospel to penetrate the heart of every person around us. Still, it is not beneath us as God's men to appreciate the artists, businessmen, poets, and athletes around us. To wonder at a scientist's intellect, enjoy a musician's composition, or rejoice at a chef's masterpiece is part of living in this world.

God as Judge

None of this suggests, however, that man is somehow sinless in his natural state. No, "*the wrath of God is revealed from heaven against all ungodliness and unrighteousness of men, who by their unrighteousness suppress the truth*" (Romans 1:18). God hates all sin and will be the ultimate judge of it. One day we will sing about His true and righteous judgments (Revelation 19:2), so when confronted with the evil of men today, we should remember God's grace toward us, but also His future judgment of all things, operating with discernment when it comes to the obvious evil around us.

Men

"Love one another with brotherly affection" (Romans 12:10).

Men regularly have no clue how to treat each other. Perhaps it is our insecurity or pride, but oftentimes our response to other men is to compete with or belittle them. At times this is done loudly, as some men boast, brag, and flaunt themselves and their successes. Quite often, however, this is done silently, as men quickly judge and dismiss other men, marginalizing them in their own minds. The man of God will have none of this and will work hard to purge these judgments, attitudes, and insecurities from his heart (Matthew 7:1). He will not become a slave to any wickedness inside his own heart, so he works hard to gain a healthy appreciation and respect for other men. If he is generally uncomfortable around other men, he sees it as a problem, something to address, and asks God to search his heart so that he can gain victory and successfully exist around other dudes (Psalm 139:23).

The man of God is thankful for other men. The ingenuity, passions, and leadership of other men in previous centuries have led to wonderful advancements, so the Christian man understands the power and potential a man possesses. He knows of the influence each man carries within his own home amongst his children and bride. He sees in each man the potential to rock and shape a community for good. Like a little boy admiring the strength of professional athletes, the godly man admires the potential and power found in other men.

Unlike so many people, the man of God refuses to make himself an island against other men (Proverbs 18:1). He wants to know men and be known by them. He may be nervous at first to speak openly and frankly with other men, but does so anyhow because he realizes the potential for growth and sharpening that could come from their wisdom (Proverbs 27:17). The godly man isn't intimidated or fearful of the insight, wisdom, and intelligence of other men, but instead chooses to pursue their counsel, thereby improving his own life and standing (Proverbs 24:6). He realizes there are such things as foolish men, so he avoids their counsel and entangling relationships with them at all costs, but still honors them and treats them respectfully (Proverbs 14:7).

The no-nonsense biblical man is fascinated by and respects men. Because he is in Christ he is secure in his own skin, so he can handle relationships with men of all shapes and sizes. Men in his community and church are seen as his fathers and brothers, so he speaks to them as such (1 Timothy 5:1). The godly man looks forward to meeting good men and allowing them to shape his life.

Women

"Many women have done excellently, but you surpass them all." (Proverbs 31:29).
"A gracious woman gets honor, and violent men get riches" (Proverbs 11:16).

It is often confusing for God's man to know how to treat women in our modern world. Poor and useless examples abound. Obviously, the man of God is not going to treat a woman like an object to be lusted after, a possession to be owned, or an incapable person to be discriminated against. Instead, the man of God is called to treat women in this world with the utmost of respect. He considers them the crowning piece of God's created order and his equal in value and position before God (Genesis 2:18). Just as Jesus is no less than equal in value to God the Father, so the woman is no less than equal in value to man (1

Corinthians 11:3). Her perspectives, opinions, and desires are valid and noteworthy. Although their roles will differ, the godly man understands the health of womanhood is important to the health of the society in general.

This honor and respect might not come naturally, however, in a world in which it is easier for a man to find an image of a naked woman than it is for him to get off the sofa and make a peanut butter and jelly sandwich. When Adam and Eve sinned, their bodies were covered, first with fig leaves and then with animal skins, but men and women have been revealing themselves ever since (Genesis 3:7, 21). While this is true, the man of God knows God has covered men and women for a reason and chooses to set his eyes only upon the naked body of his wife (Proverbs 5:15-21). The man of God realizes that exposure to pornography and Victoria's Secret commercials can work subversively and negatively on his attitude toward women, so for this and many other reasons, he refuses to go there. Because his eye is a gateway to his heart, the man of God guards it with everything within him (Matthew 6:22-23).

On top of all this, the godly man sees women in this world as a wonderful counterpart to what men bring to the table. Their creativity, expertise, and passions may not be shared by him, but are valued by him. In his church, school, city, and workplace the man of God sees women as his sisters and mothers (1 Timothy 5:2). Instead of speaking down to them, he exalts them with his speech and behavior. Instead of treating them like one of the boys, he chooses to act in a dignified manner around them. Instead of speaking callously and bluntly to them, as he might to one of his male friends, he speaks with deference and esteem. He's learned that punching, wrestling, and the sounds that accompany bodily functions are to be reserved for his friendships with other guys.

The man of God will not be a flirtatious poser. He will not tease a woman by pretending interest, but since she is his sister, he will instead guard her heart and his by being a man of integrity. If he is interested and ready to pursue a relationship, he will take the lead and pursue her. He will not let his insecurity dictate the terms and force him to wait to see "if she likes me" or any other such nonsense.

If by the grace of God, a man finds himself in a dating relationship or with a girlfriend at some point in his life, he will not move in with her or have her move in with him. He knows that if breaking off a dating relationship means that you pack up your clothes, furniture, and toothbrush, then it will be all too easy to divorce after marriage because it will feel exactly the same as a breakup. He will treat her with the honor and dignity he would give to his little sister. If they plan to marry, he will honor her by waiting to enjoy her body until the day of their wedding.

The man of God will not be dismissive of women. Although they are different from him, he cannot imagine life without them. He will consider women his friends, although in a different light and manner than his male friends. He will protect, lead, and serve. He will strive to be a blessing to the better half.

Children

"The righteous man who walks in his integrity—blessed are his children after him!" (Proverbs 20:7).

While selfish and foolish men may see children as a nuisance or a hindrance, the godly man sees children as a blessing and a heritage from God (Psalm 127:3). He realizes these children will grow to be mothers and fathers and leaders and influencers, so they are people who need to be mentored now. Just as he sees enormous potential in other men, the godly man sees enormous potential in every single child. The godly man does not ignore or marginalize children, but instead gives them the honor that is their due. Most importantly, he sees them as worthy of receiving Christ and lives his life in a way that would encourage them to know Jesus (Matthew 19:14).

As his own children, the godly man takes time to listen and cultivate a relationship with the children of others. Just as our Heavenly Father does not want a one-way dialogue with us, in which He directs and speaks to us without any response from us to Him, so a good father wants to speak to and be spoken to, by his children (Matthew 6:9); but the godly man also enjoys listening to the children of others.

Understanding that children need to see examples of what real men are like, the godly man will look children in the eye, shake their hands, and ask them questions in order to get to know them. He is not above reading them books, playing with them, or sitting as the audience of their performances. While it may be fashionable for some children to roll their eyes at grown-ups, he does not think it is fashionable for a grown-up man to roll his eyes at children. In other words, he understands they are children, so they aren't fully developed spiritually, mentally, or emotionally. Instead of being exasperated by them, he is patient with them and willing to be involved in the nurturing process.

The godly man is an excellent coach or mentor or teacher to children of all ages. He constantly has a vision for each one of them. He sees potential for the men and women they could become if they give themselves to hard work and dedication. He encourages the best out of them. He is an excellent teacher of children and finds joy in so doing. On top of this, he is the kind of man children should observe.

He isn't an immoral man with backward priorities, basically a boy in a grown man's body, but is different. He is unlike one coach I had who loved to talk of his sexual escapades and drunken adventures, impressing teenage boys in the process. On the contrary, he is a man who is interested in the lives of the kids around him. They will observe his respect for authority, love for his wife, and devotion to his children, and they will be better for it.

Church

"Obey your leaders and submit to them, for they are keeping watch over your souls, as those who will have to give an account. Let them do this with joy and not with groaning, for that would be of no advantage to you" (Hebrews 13:17).

The man of God, simply put, is a churchman. He doesn't simply attend church; this would never be enough for him. Instead, he wants to serve, be known, know others, and grow in his walk with Christ. If gifted and called as a leader, he longs to lead, but not before he longs to submit and follow. He is not like the man who drove his family from church to church because he couldn't find a church to his liking or a pastor who would submit to him, but is instead a man who finds a solid church and faithfully supports the leadership of that church. If the church leadership is operating in a biblical, ethical, and moral way, he gets behind them and trusts them as they lead the fellowship.

This man understands that the church is the bride of Christ, so she must be well loved by Jesus. Because Jesus loves her and shed his blood in order to obtain her, this man also adores the church and has a deep and profound love for it. He understands the church is never going to be a perfect organization here on earth, but is instead going through a purification process which will be consummated on the great day of the Lord.

Consequently, this man is not looking for the perfect church. He looks for a church that honors Christ and His word by proclaiming the Gospel and communicating scripture. He cheers for the church and is an active participant in it, praying for the leadership, giving faithfully to the work, and serving on a regular basis in areas he is passionate for. Over time, this man will become a pillar in his home church. People will begin to see him and his family as exemplary and worthy of imitation.

This man is faithful to his church and can be counted on by his church. He regularly attends services, Bible studies, and small groups. He knows God is everywhere at all times, but he also knows God is present when His people gather in a special way. Because of this, and because of his deep desire to minister to God and others through worship and service, this man is faithful to participate in his local fellowship. He wonders what he can bring to the church rather than what he can get from the church. He brings a servant's mentality to church, and does "*nothing from selfish ambition or conceit, but in humility count others more significant than (himself)*" (Philippians 2:3).

When this man falls into sin, he is quick to confess it to his brothers in the church (1 John 1:9). If there is a chance his sin might disqualify him from any work or ministry he is currently involved in within the church, he will especially communicate his sin to the leaders, submitting to their judgment on the matter (Hebrews 13:17). This comes naturally for him because church is a place where he is known. He isn't a secret attender or a man who lives in the shadows of the church, but has instead chosen to become a part of the very fabric of the body.

Government

"Let every person be subject to the governing authorities. For there is no authority except from God, and those that exist have been instituted by God" (Romans 13:1).

The godly man understands that the church can flourish under any political system. What he longs for—more than any outward political change—is internal change of heart within a nation's people. He is more concerned for the success of the Gospel than his political ideology.

That said, the man of God understands that it is God who has instituted and stands behind human forms of government. Because man is made in the image of God, the godly man knows that in the past, God had required the life of anyone who took the life of another, thereby instituting a human institution of justice or government (Genesis 9:5–6). He knows that, ideally, the government *"is the servant of God, an avenger who carries out God's wrath on the wrongdoer"* (Romans 13:4). He understands this justice system is never carried out perfectly, but looks forward to the day when God will justly judge the world. In the meantime, he prays for kings, governors, and those who are in authority because they have a really complicated job to do (1 Timothy 2:2).

He listens to words like Peter's: *"Be subject for the Lord's sake to every human institution, whether it be to the emperor as supreme, or to governors as sent by him to punish those who do evil and to praise those who do good"* (1 Peter 2:13–14). He knows Peter and the rest of the early church did not live in ideal political situations, but were heavily persecuted by their government.

Still, the man of God does what he can within the context of his political system and determines to never disobey God in his obedience to his earthly leaders (Acts 5:27-29). Like Daniel before him, if his government forbids his worship, he will disobey his government and bend the knee to his God. Like a child who honors his parents even when they aren't very honorable people, the man of God honors the governmental leaders because of the office they occupy and the institution they are in.

Honor Others

"Outdo one another in showing honor" (Romans 12:10).

This man honors those he is responsible to and responsible for. He honors everyone around him. Like Jesus before him, his honor of others does not dilute his message in the least. No, he speaks the truth with love in his heart, but honor exudes from his life. He respects people, admires people, and attempts to find the best in people. Where his submission is required, he gives it. He is an honorable man who freely shows honor to the people around him. This man is a rich blessing to the people he comes into contact with. I would encourage you to cultivate this kind of attitude.

The other day I walked into one of our local batting cages establishments in order to sign up one of my daughters for softball. I had determined ahead of time to be courteous, thankful, and respectful to everyone there, especially by taking the time to honor the men who had devoted years to building up the local league. I'm not sure if they are believers or not, but it seemed right to thank and honor them for their service to our community and children. This kind of heart can follow us wherever we go. Coworkers, cashiers, and coaches should feel honored by us. We believe they are made in the image of God, so because God's love for them runs deep, and perhaps for no other reason, we will honor them.

Be Thankful

I am very thankful for the variety and diversity of people in my life. God has put wonderful men, women, and children around me, people who have been made in the image of God, but who are also far different from me. It is good for the man of God to appreciate and grow in thankfulness for these differences in people.

I lean toward being an introvert. I love and appreciate others and can admire the diversity of styles and personalities, but I more naturally lean toward isolation. I enjoy hiking, reading, and endurance sports where I spend long amounts of time in solitude. It is not hard for me to be left alone. Perhaps this is why I spent my time writing a book! That said, I am very thankful for God, His word, and His church. I am thankful for others and am glad I am not alone. Without the work of God's grace in my heart, I think my natural tendency toward aloneness would have produced an ugly kind of man. Instead, I have been encouraged by God's Spirit and His word time and time again to involve myself with others. I find myself richly rewarded by the experience, not that a reward has been my goal. I simply wanted to obey my God and serve Him, but He has in turn used these relationships in my life to shape and mold me for the better. To God be the glory!

Chapter 8: Your Hope

"Have I not commanded you? Be strong and courageous. Do not be frightened, and do not be dismayed, for the Lord your God is with you wherever you go" (Joshua 1:9).

This life can seem incredibly daunting at times. As a man, there is a temptation to grow tired and depressed when it comes to our progress and transformation. Be not discouraged. God is with you. Discouragement is the weapon of our enemy who loves to discourage us in order to introduce us to temptation, sin, and death. Instead, realize the wonderful hope that is yours in Jesus Christ. He is a friend like no other, a friend who has committed to go with you and fight for you in this life. He has promised to go with you as you step out in obedience to Him (Matthew 28:20).

Still, there are times this life is absolutely overwhelming. Our threshold should increase over time, but at each stage of life, there are different pressures which could easily derail us in our pursuit of God and His kingdom.

I remember one such season of pressure early on in my walk with God. Without getting into the details, at one point during my college years, I had begun to feel an immense burden as I considered some of the coming crossroads of my life. The responsibilities of that hour seem like nothing to me now, but they were very heavy upon me as I went through it. I was distressed and perplexed as to what the future would or should hold. The confidence, assurance, and hope that is mine in Christ was conspicuously absent from my heart. In short, I was stressed out and worried about my future. I wondered how I would ever make it.

One day I was studying the book and life of Joshua for a little Bible study I had been teaching to middle school students. I had followed Joshua as he took leadership in Israel, sent the two spies into Jericho to determine the mood of the Canaanites, and miraculously crossed the Jordan River with the people. I had seen how God had closed up the river behind them, commanded the men to become circumcised like Abraham before them, and withheld the manna from them; instead commanding them to eat of the fruit of the land.

As I studied, I wondered at the intense pressure Joshua could have felt as he led the people. On this particular day, I came to Joshua 5:13–15, a moment *"when Joshua was by Jericho."* I imagined him there, planning, plotting, and perhaps stressing over the future of Israel. How could they ever defeat Jericho, a fortified city? God had told them they would be able to defeat Jericho, but never before had they been next to this city, a city which typified the great battles sure to follow. How would or could they ever defeat this Canaanite people?

Indeed, this was the first time Joshua and Israel had been next to Jericho. They had previously always been across from or opposite Jericho, but never before had they been beside it. This was new. Joshua, along with his entire nation, had never experienced this before. I imagined a great weight overcoming Joshua's heart. He was leading in Moses's stead. The glorious victory at the Jordan River had begun to fade. It was getting real, fast. They were about to go to war.

Joshua had experienced a lot of God's grace and favor up to that point in his life. He had submitted to God and fought the Amalekites under Moses's direction (Exodus 17). He had stayed in the tabernacle to receive the afterglow of God's presence after Moses's meetings with God (Exodus 33:11). He had believed in God, along with Caleb, even though the rest of the spies lacked the faith required to go into the promised land forty years earlier (Numbers 14:6). He had been trained through Moses's commands and encouragements, making him a man full of the wisdom of God (Deuteronomy 1, 3, 34:9). Still, this was an entirely new moment in Joshua's life. He had never led the people into battle against Jericho. I imagined a deep pressure invading his heart.

Perhaps you've felt this way before. You've sensed a deep burden and pressure during some new season in your life. As I sat there studying Joshua's life, I felt like I was tasting perhaps a little piece of the pressure he must have been experiencing. I didn't know how I would get through the next stretch of my life. I didn't have a massive and fortified city in front of me, but I sure felt like it. The questions regarding my future seemed worse to me than any Jericho, mostly because I knew how the Jericho story ended, but I had no idea how my story would conclude.

As I read on, I discovered a man who appeared in front of Joshua with his sword in his hand. Joshua immediately wanted to know, "*Are you for us, or for our adversaries?*" (Joshua 5:13). The sight of a warrior with his sword drawn was disconcerting to Joshua. If this fighter was on Israel's side, why did he have his weapon at the ready? Joshua hadn't given any orders, much less developed a plan of attack. If he was on Jericho's side, it was time to rumble. Joshua pressed this man to reveal his allegiances.

Instead of choosing one of two sides, Israel or Jericho, this man merely revealed his true nature. He said, "*No; but I am the commander of the army of the Lord. Now I have come*" (Joshua 5:14). He first indicated his military affiliation. He wasn't with the army of Jericho or the army of Israel, but the army of God. Secondly, he told Joshua that he wasn't just in the army of God, but was the actual commander of that army. The Lord was appearing to Joshua, letting him know of His presence in Joshua's life. He, not Joshua, would do the fighting. He, not Joshua, would create the battle plan. He, not Joshua, would give the victory.

As I read on in the story, I appreciated Joshua's response. *"Joshua fell on his face to the earth and worshiped and said to him, 'What does my lord say to his servant?"* (Joshua 5:14). When I read this at that stage of my life, I sensed a major burden being lifted off Joshua's heart because a major burden was being lifted off of mine. I imagined Joshua's heart leaping for joy at the reality that he wasn't the one responsible for the nation—God was. God would fight for them. God would go with them. I imagined Joshua, a man who was laboring and heavily laden, finding the rest of God as found in Christ (Matthew 11:28). As I read Joshua's story, I felt God telling me more of my story. I sensed Him releasing me of the burden. He would fight for me. He would lead my life.

What follows in Joshua's life is remarkable. The Lord gave him an otherworldly plan to defeat the city of Jericho. Conspicuously absent were the strategies and marks of traditional warfare in God's plan for the people to encircle the city once a day for six days, and on the seventh day, to encircle it seven times. After some trumpets and some shouting, the walls would collapse, and the victory would be theirs. I often laugh as I imagine Joshua explaining this plan to his leadership. They had seen God do some amazing things, but this was crazy!

Upon reading of the victory God gave Israel over Jericho, I realized one simple truth. God's plans and leadership over my life wouldn't always be conventional. He is the God of the impossible, so He would lead my life in ways that might seem impossible to me. He would create a battle plan and strategy that was otherworldly, but incredibly effective. Once I recognized this, a great release occurred within my heart. I slowly began to trust God more, rejoicing that the burden was not mine to bear. I wanted to be an available vessel for Him to use, but by design and of necessity, the victory could only come through Him. The unseen armies of God would grant me victory. I have watched God fight on my behalf ever since.

The victory is found "*Not by might, nor by power, but by my Spirit, says the Lord of hosts*" (Zechariah 4:6). God is the one who will enable you to become the man of God you long to be. There will be difficulties, setbacks, and obstacles, but this life can only be lived by the grace and power of God. "*Cast your burden on the Lord, and he will sustain you; he will never permit the righteous to be moved*" (Psalm 55:22).

Perhaps your weight is heavy. Perhaps you have lived contrary to the wisdom found in God's word for so long that your life has become an absolute mess. Maybe you are so discouraged or fearful you can't imagine how you could move forward from this point. Maybe you are contemplating a future step of faith and it feels very uncertain to you.

Know that you aren't alone. God went with Joshua, David, the apostles, and many others. God will go with you. He loves you and has a plan for your life. It might be unconventional, and you might have a long road in front of you, but it is good.

Maybe you are paralyzed by fear, much like Elisha's servant when the armies of Syria came to fight against his master. Elisha attempted to comfort him by saying, "*Do not be afraid, for those who are with us are more than those who are with them*" (2 Kings 6:16). Then Elisha prayed, "'*O Lord, please open his eyes that he may see.' So the Lord opened the eyes of the young man, and he saw, and behold, the mountain was full of horses and chariots of fire all around Elisha*" (2 Kings 6:17). Only after his eyes were opened, was this young man released of his burdens and fear.

My prayer for you is that your eyes would be opened to the grace, power, and strength of God. He is more than able. I long for you to *"have strength to comprehend with all the saints what is the breadth and length and height and depth, and to know the love of Christ that surpasses knowledge, that you may be filled with all the fullness of God"* (Ephesians 3:18–19). When our eyes are opened to the wonderful grace and power of God as found in Christ, we are changed. Peace, boldness, and confidence rush into our hearts, ingredients that are necessary for a man to excel.

Please persist in walking with God. Your world and life are in such need. The people around you need to see Christ. Be His messenger, His hands, and His feet. Demonstrate the love of Christ to the world around you. God is looking for men like you. He is searching for men who will honor Him, trust Him, and obey Him. He is looking for men who will radically impact this world before entering a glorious eternity with Him. He is looking for men of courage and boldness, men who will fearlessly and relentlessly pursue God and His kingdom at all costs. He is looking for humble men who will tenderly love the people God has placed in His life. He is looking for men who have been rocked by the truth of the Gospel and the precious blood of Christ. He is looking for men of integrity and passion, availability and zeal. He is calling you. He is looking for you. Answer His glorious call. Your life will never be the same.

Acknowledgments

I hope you have been encouraged and strengthened by God through this book. I would like to especially acknowledge my father, Bill Holdridge, who demonstrated and taught me so many of the principles found within this book (and for whom my middle initial stands!). I would also like to acknowledge the church and staff of Calvary Monterey for its love and support of our family and ministry work. Additionally, I want to thank my wife, Christina, for her patience and encouragement in every season of our wonderful marriage. Lastly, I want to tell my daughters how much I love them. Thank you for reading.

- Nate

For more information on this book or its author, including speaking engagements and audio teachings, please contact us at nateholdridge.com.

18850503R00087

Made in the USA
Charleston, SC
24 April 2013